Plessy v. Ferguson

Separate but Equal

FAMOUS TRIALS

Plessy v. Ferguson
Separate but Equal

Other books in the Famous Trials series:

Plessy v. Ferguson
Separate but Equal

by Nathan Aaseng

FAMOUS TRIALS

LUCENT BOOKS®

THOMSON

™

GALE

San Diego • Detroit • New York • San Francisco • Cleveland
New Haven, Conn. • Waterville, Maine • London • Munich

LIBRARY OF CONGRESS CATALOGING-IN-PUBLICATION DATA

Aaseng, Nathan
   Plessy v. Ferguson / by Nathan Aaseng
      p. cm. — (Famous trials)
Summary: Profiles the 1896 Supreme Court trial that tested the constitutionality of
laws in the South that enforced racial segregation in train travel, and discusses the
impact of the verdict which provided a legal cover for racial discrimination throughout
the United States.
Includes bibliographical references and index.
   ISBN 1-59018-268-5 (hardback : alk. paper)
   1. Plessy, Homer Adolph — Trials, litigation, etc. — Juvenile literature. 2. Segregation in transportation — Law and legislation — Louisiana — History — Juvenile literature. 3. Segregation — Law and legislation — United States — History — Juvenile
literature. 4. United States — Race relations — History — Juvenile literature. [1. Plessy,
Homer Adolph — Trials, litigation, etc. 2. Segregation in transprotation — Law and legislation. 3. Segregation — Law and legislation. 4. Race relations — History. 5. African
Americans — Civil rights — History.] I. Title: Plessy v. Ferguson. II. Title. III. Series.
   KF223.P56A15 2003
   342.73'0873—dc21

                                      2003000410

Table of Contents

Foreword

"The law is not an end in and of itself, nor does it provide ends. It is preeminently a means to serve what we think is right."

William J. Brennan Jr.

THE CONCEPT OF JUSTICE AND THE RULE OF LAW are hallmarks of Western civilization, manifested perhaps most visibly in widely famous and dramatic court trials. These trials include such important and memorable personages as the ancient Greek philosopher Socrates, who was accused and convicted of corrupting the minds of his society's youth in 399 B.C.; the French maiden and military leader Joan of Arc, accused and convicted of heresy against the church in 1431; to former football star O.J. Simpson, acquitted of double murder in 1995. These and other well-known and controversial trials constitute the most public, and therefore most familiar, demonstrations of a Western legal tradition that dates back through the ages. Although no one is certain when the first law code appeared or when the first formal court trials were held, Babylonian ruler Hammurabi introduced the first known law code in about 1760 B.C. It remains unclear how this code was administered, and no records of specific trials have survived. What is clear, however, is that humans have always sought to govern behavior and define actions in terms of law.

Almost all societies have made laws and prosecuted people for going against those laws, but the question of which behaviors to sanction and which to censure has always been controversial and remains in flux. Some, such as Roman orator and legislator Cicero, argue that laws are simply applications of universal standards. Cicero believed that humanity would agree on what constituted illegal behavior and that human laws were a mere extension of natural laws. "True law is right reason in agreement with nature," he wrote,

8

world-wide in scope, unchanging, everlasting. . . . We may not oppose or alter that law, we cannot abolish it, we cannot be freed from its obligations by any legislature. . . .This [natural] law does not differ for Rome and for Athens, for the present and for the future. . . . It is and will be valid for all nations and all times.

Cicero's rather optimistic view has been contradicted throughout history, however. For every law made to preserve harmony and set universal standards of behavior, another has been born of fear, prejudice, greed, desire for power, and a host of other motives. History is replete with individuals defying and fighting to change such laws—and even to topple governments that dictate such laws. Abolitionists fought against slavery, civil rights leaders fought for equal rights, millions throughout the world have fought for independence—these constitute a minimum of reasons for which people have sought to overturn laws that they believed to be wrong or unjust. In opposition to Cicero, then, many others, such as eighteenth-century English poet and philosopher William Godwin, believe humans must be constantly vigilant against bad laws. As Godwin said in 1793:

Laws we sometimes call the wisdom of our ancestors. But this is a strange imposition. It was as frequently the dictate of their passion, of timidity, jealousy, a monopolizing spirit, and a lust of power that knew no bounds. Are we not obliged perpetually to renew and remodel this misnamed wisdom of our ancestors? To correct it by a detection of their ignorance, and a censure of their intolerance?

Lucent Books' *Famous Trials* series showcases trials that exemplify both society's praiseworthy condemnation of universally unacceptable behavior, and its misguided persecution of individuals based on fear and ignorance, as well as trials that leave open the question of whether justice has been done. Each volume begins by setting the scene and providing a historical context to show how society's mores influence the trial process and the verdict.

Each book goes on to present a detailed and lively account of the trial, including liberal use of primary source material such as direct testimony, lawyers' summations, and contemporary and modern commentary. In addition, sidebars throughout the text create a broader context by presenting illuminating details about important points of law, information on key personalities, and important distinctions related to civil, federal, and criminal procedures. Thus, all of the primary and secondary source material included in both the text and the sidebars demonstrates to readers the sources and methods historians use to derive information and conclusions about such events.

Lastly, each *Famous Trials* volume includes one or more of the following comprehensive tools that motivate readers to pursue further reading and research. A timeline allows readers to see the scope of the trial at a glance, annotated bibliographies provide both sources for further research and a thorough list of works consulted, a glossary helps students with unfamiliar words and concepts, and a comprehensive index permits quick scanning of the book as a whole.

The insight of Oliver Wendell Holmes Jr., distinguished Supreme Court justice, exemplifies the theme of the *Famous Trials* series. Taken from *The Common Law*, published in 1881, Holmes remarked: "The life of the law has not been logic, it has been experience." That "experience" consists mainly in how laws are applied in society and challenged in the courts, a process resulting in differing outcomes from one generation to the next. Thus, the *Famous Trials* series encourages readers to examine trials within a broader historical and social context.

Introduction

A Short but Historic Trip

HOMER ADOLPH PLESSY knew he was taking a big risk as he approached the ticket counter of the East Louisiana Railway on June 7, 1892. If the white citizens of New Orleans knew what the thirty-four-year-old shoemaker was up to, there was a good chance he could end up with a severe beating, or worse.

Homer Plessy bought a train ticket in New Orleans, Louisiana (pictured in the late nineteenth century). He sat in the first-class section reserved for whites and was arrested for refusing to move to the "colored" car.

Plessy stepped up to the window and purchased a first-class ticket for the short train trip to Covington, Louisiana, on the other side of the lake. But even as he boarded the train, he had no intention of traveling to Covington, or even of leaving New Orleans. Instead, he was setting in motion a carefully scripted drama designed to land him in jail. The well-dressed Plessy deliberately walked to the first-class coach reserved for white travelers and found a vacant seat. As the train left the station, the conductor came into the coach and asked Plessy if he was "colored," a common term for someone who was at least partly of the black race.

The question might have seemed odd, even shocking, to an observer. Plessy appeared for all the world to be white; there was nothing about his appearance to make him out of place in the whites-only car. But one of his great-grandparents had been black and that was enough to classify him in the South as "colored," and thus a member of an inferior race. The conductor had asked about his racial background only because he had been tipped off. In fact Plessy had sat in a coach reserved for whites on other trips without attracting any attention.

In answering the conductor's question, the shoemaker responded that he was indeed colored, whereupon he was asked to leave his seat and move to the section reserved for blacks. Plessy politely refused. The conductor then summoned a police officer who forcibly removed Plessy from the train and escorted him to the New Orleans jail.

The Case Goes to Court

Plessy was charged with violating a recently passed Louisiana law that stated, "All railway companies carrying passengers in their coaches in this state shall provide equal but separate accommodations for the white, and colored races, by providing two or more passenger coaches for each train. No person or persons shall be permitted to occupy seats in coaches, other than the ones assigned to them, on account of the race they belong to."[1] The penalty for violating this law had been set at a twenty-five-dollar fine or twenty days in jail.

Segregation laws were in place in the South, requiring separate facilities for blacks and whites. The shop pictured above is an example of a "colored only" facility.

The law placed upon the officers of the train the responsibility of enforcing the law. It specified penalties for "refusal or neglect of the officers, directors, conductors, and employees of railway companies to comply with the act."[2] Thus, a conductor who failed to discriminate against his passengers on the basis of race could be fined or jailed.

Plessy and his lawyers argued before Judge John Howard Ferguson in New Orleans Parish Criminal Court that the case should be thrown out because the law was an unconstitutional violation of Plessy's rights as a U.S. citizen. In one of many ironic twists of fate that would accompany the trial, Ferguson had been a Massachusetts lawyer before moving to New Orleans. This Northerner from what had been the strongest antislavery state in the nation disagreed with Plessy's arguments and found him guilty of the criminal act.

A National Test Case

Rather than being outraged or disappointed, Plessy and his lawyers were satisfied. The entire episode had been carefully arranged to produce just such a result. Plessy was a member of a group of New Orleans blacks known as the Citizens Committee to Test the Constitutionality of the Separate Car Law. Their goal had been to bring about a test case that would force the nation's highest courts to rule on whether the law was valid under the rules of the U.S. Constitution. Plessy had been chosen to challenge the law precisely because of his appearance, which pointed up the absurdity of making laws discriminating between races.

Ferguson's rejection of Plessy's defense gave Plessy and his lawyers a chance to appeal the matter to higher courts, which could decide once and for all whether such discriminatory laws were legal. As the case worked its way up the court system on appeal it was known as *Plessy versus Ferguson* or often shortened to *Plessy v. Ferguson*, because Plessy was challenging Judge Ferguson's ruling.

Plessy v. Ferguson produced one of the worst verdicts in the history of the Supreme Court, a verdict that would have far-reaching, devastating effects on U.S. society.

Chapter 1

Freed but Equal?

LOUISIANA'S SEPARATE CAR LAW was one of a series of laws that the former states of the Confederacy passed with increasing frequency in the final decades of the nineteenth century to promote an official policy of separation between the white and black races. These laws and this policy had their roots in the institution of slavery which had been widespread in the South and present as well in the North at the founding of the United States.

Separation of Races

As twentieth-century Supreme Court justice Warren Burger observed, "separation of the races is inherent in any system of race-based slavery."[3] The entitlement of one race to own members of another can be recognized only in a society that accepts stark distinctions between the races and holds one to be superior to the other. This was the case at the founding of the United States. Despite the lofty words of the Declaration of Independence that "all men are created equal and endowed by their creator with certain inalienable rights,"[4] the U.S. Constitution did not consider all men equal, designating slaves as three-fifths of a person for purposes of census counts to determine the number of representatives in government.

Feelings among whites toward blacks in the early United States ranged from a scattered few who considered blacks the equal of whites to those who agreed with U.S. vice president John C. Calhoun, a South Carolinan who argued that blacks were so intellectually inferior that they could never be educated and

15

that slavery was the best thing for them. The prevailing notion, in the North as well as the South, was that the races were indeed unequal and that even free blacks should not mingle with whites in many social situations. In the 1830s, for example, a Connecticut mob destroyed a school that had admitted black students, and the state legislature passed a law forbidding the establishment of schools for free Negroes. Historian C. Vann Woodward sums up the situation by writing, "Denied full rights and privileges of citizens, deprived of equality in the courts, and restricted in their freedom of movements, the so-called free Negro [prior to the Civil War] shared many of the deprivations of the slave. In addition, measures of ostracism were leveled at members of this class to emphasize their status."[5]

A slave family poses outside their home. Since the founding of the United States, blacks had been regarded as an inferior race.

The End of Slavery

Although most Americans believed that whites were superior to blacks, many of them grew uncomfortable with the idea of humans owning other humans. In the first half of the nineteenth century, the nation became engaged in an increasingly heated political dispute, largely divided along North and South lines, over whether the ownership of African slaves was morally proper.

The Supreme Court tried to settle the dispute once and for all in its ruling in the *Dred Scott* case in 1857. By a 7-2 vote, the Court ruled that Scott, the slave of a deceased man, had no right to sue his former master's estate for his freedom even though Scott had lived for a time in a state in which slavery was not legal. Speaking for the Court, Chief Justice Roger Taney attempted to define the standing of blacks in U.S. society. He wrote that blacks could not become U.S. citizens because, in his view, the Constitution never intended to include them as such, and therefore they had "no rights which the white man was bound to respect."[6] Furthermore, Taney ruled that states could not prohibit slavery because this would be an infringement of the individual's right to own property.

Taney's ruling was so extreme that it provoked a storm of outrage in parts of the North. The status of blacks, both slave and free, became an explosive political issue. A strong abolitionist movement, centered in Massachusetts, grew in the North. Debate over the status of blacks became a key campaign issue. In the Illinois senate race of 1858, Stephen Douglas, running for reelection against Abraham Lincoln, laid out his position, which reflected the stance of the national Democratic Party:

> I am opposed to taking any step that recognizes the Negro man or the Indian as the equal of the white man. I am opposed to giving him a voice in the administration of the government. I would extend to the Negro, and the Indian, and to all dependent races every right, every privilege, and every immunity consistent with the safety

THE DREADFUL *DRED SCOTT* DECISION

The U.S. Supreme Court's boldest statement regarding the rights of African Americans prior to the Civil War came in the *Dred Scott* case. Scott was the slave of army doctor John Emerson, whose travels had brought the two men to the states of Illinois and Wisconsin, where slavery was not allowed.

In 1846, three years after Emerson's death, Scott sued Emerson's estate for his freedom, claiming that under Missouri law a slave who set up residency in a free state was declared free. The case dragged slowly through the courts and it was not until 1850 that he won his case in Missouri. The case was then appealed to the U.S. Supreme Court, where the wheels of justice ground even more slowly. On March 6, 1857, the Court handed down a ruling that sparked a furious reaction in the Northern states. In a 7-2 decision, the Court declared that Scott had no right to sue for anything in the U.S. courts because he was not a citizen of the United States.

The Court's opinion, written by seventy-year-old Chief Justice Roger Taney of the slave state of Maryland, not only refused to accept Scott's plea but appeared to many to go out of its way to antagonize the North with comments about the "inferiority of Negroes" and by saying that the states had no legal right to interfere with the rights of citizens to own property in the form of slaves. The Court's decision outraged Northerners and increased the mounting hostility between sections of the country. Meanwhile, thousands of free blacks in the North fled to Canada, Mexico, and Haiti for fear that they would be captured and enslaved by Southerners.

The Supreme Court ruled against Dred Scott in his suit for his freedom.

Taney's contempt for African Americans ran deep. Unapologetic for the furor he had caused, Taney later said, "The African race in the United States, even when free, are everywhere a degraded class and exercise no political influence. The privileges they are allowed to enjoy are accorded to them as a matter of kindness and benevolence rather than right."

The *Dred Scott* decision has been widely denounced as one of the worst decisions the Supreme Court has ever made.

and welfare of the white races: but equality they never should have, either political or social, or in any other respect whatever.[7]

On January 1, 1863, in the midst of the terrible Civil War sparked in part by the slavery issue, President Abraham Lincoln's Emancipation Proclamation declared all slaves in the South free. The momentum against slavery swelled until on January 31, 1865, the House of Representatives passed the Thirteenth Amendment to the Constitution. This amendment, which outlawed slavery throughout the United States, was ratified by the states and went into effect on December 18 of that year.

What Will the New Society Look Like?

The end of slavery left the nation with a new problem: how to restructure American society to accommodate the sudden change in status of roughly 4 million blacks. Blacks were now free, but were they equal? As before the Civil War, Americans held a wide range of views on this issue. There was a strong but vocal group that believed in equality of the races. Even among those who did not hold such views, few in the North agreed with Taney's decree that blacks had no rights that whites were bound to respect. There was a widespread feeling that fair treatment of blacks required the nation to grant them a large measure of protection under the laws.

But the consensus remained that the black and white races were not equal. Typical of those who were convinced that the races were unequal was Democratic senator John T. Morgan of Alabama, who said, "The inferiority of the negro race, as compared with the white race, is so essentially true, and so obvious, that to assume it in argument cannot be justly attributed to prejudice."[8] Such views were not confined to the Deep South. In the 1860s Delaware's state senate passed a resolution stating, "The immutable laws of God have affixed upon the brow of the white race the ineffaceable stamp of superiority."[9] Similar claims that the superior position of whites was ordained by God further cemented the conviction that blacks were inferior.

This left the United States with a complicated problem. Could it fashion a nation in which the two races could live together as equals under the law while one was held to be socially unequal to the other? Many doubted this was possible, much less desirable. Even Thomas Jefferson, who publicly expressed his moral objections to slavery, believed that blacks and whites were by nature so different that it would be impossible to create a society in which the two existed side by side as equals. Any attempt to do so, he wrote, "will probably never end but in the extermination of the one or the other race."[10] As late as 1865 only six states in the entire nation had granted blacks the right to vote.

The Black Codes

Many of the former Confederate states were not willing to try to include freed slaves in their social structure. No sooner did the war end than their legislatures and local governing bodies began enacting laws designed to keep the former slaves humble and impoverished.

The repressive laws passed by the former Confederate states became known as the Black Codes. One notorious Black Code tactic was to convict a black of some petty crime and then levy a large fine as punishment. Since few former slaves had any money, those accused were seldom able to pay these fines. They were then labeled "vagrants" and sentenced to hard labor in order to pay off their debt. In effect they were sent back into slavery.

Black Code laws banned blacks from testifying in court against whites or serving on juries, which opened them up to a host of injustices. They had no recourse when whites cheated them or stole from them. In many towns blacks could not enter without written permission and were not allowed to stay overnight. Black Code laws prohibited Negroes from assembling in a group for any reason without a white person present. Blacks were banned from most shops, hotels, restrooms, and many forms of public transportation; in Georgia, Arkansas, and Texas blacks could not legally attend any school.

Former slaves like these were impacted by Black Codes, laws passed in the South that denied many basic rights to blacks.

In addition to these legal actions were behaviors clearly outside the law. There were news reports of riots in Tennessee and other states in 1866 in which mobs of heavily armed whites began firing at any blacks they came across. Historian James W. Loewen reports, "In Hinds County, Mississippi, alone, whites killed an average of one African American a day, many of them servicemen, during Confederate Reconstruction—the period from 1865 to 1867."[11] In Louisiana more than one thousand people, mostly African Americans, were murdered in the summer and fall of 1868.

Furious Reaction in the North

When stories about the Black Codes reached the North, even those who had not been enthusiastic supporters of black rights grew furious. Many of their family members, friends, and neighbors had given their lives in the recently ended Civil War to preserve the

OPPOSITION TO BLACKS IN EDUCATION

Segregation of schools in the early nineteenth-century United States was not strictly a Southern phenomenon. Prior to the 1830s, blacks were simply not allowed in schools attended by whites. In 1834 Henry Highland Garnet, Alexander Crummell, and a few other promising black students took part in a bold experiment in integrated education at the Noyes Academy in New Hampshire. During the summer, however, the townspeople destroyed the school and surrounded a house where the black students were living. Garnet dispersed them with a musket shot but the townspeople then dragged the ruined schoolhouse into a swamp a half mile away.

The first significant court challenge to segregated education came in 1849, when Sarah Roberts sued the city of Boston for denying her child the right to attend a public school reserved for whites. Attorney Charles Sumner, later a U.S. senator and one of the most impassioned abolitionists in the nation, argued that the city's system of separate schools for the races violated the child's rights under the state constitution. Sumner claimed that the schools for blacks were inferior and, using an argument that would be echoed a half century later in *Plessy v. Ferguson*, said that the system of segregation stigmatized all blacks as inferior as well.

Abolitionist Charles Sumner argued against segregation of schools.

The Massachusetts Supreme Court ruled against Roberts and upheld the city's segregation policy. However, public opinion in the state shifted so dramatically over the next few years that in 1855 the Massachusetts legislature made it illegal to exclude anyone from a public school on grounds of race or religion. In this, Massachusetts and other parts of the North broke from the South, where segregation in public schools was set in stone.

Union and abolish slavery. Now it appeared that the former Confederate states were refusing to acknowledge that they had lost the war and were trying to return blacks to their former position of servitude. Northerners were incensed at the idea that their loved ones had died in vain. An editorial in the *Chicago Tribune* thundered, "The men of the North will convert the state of Mississippi into a frog pond before they will allow any such laws to disgrace one foot of soil in which the bones of our soldiers sleep and over which the flag of freedom waves."[12]

Congress, under the leadership of Representative Thaddeus Stevens of Pennsylvania, immediately responded with dramatic legislative and executive actions to combat the Black Codes, thus beginning an era known as the Reconstruction. The "Act to Protect All Persons in the United States in Their Civil Rights" specifically declared African Americans to be citizens and decreed that no state could deny to any citizen the equal protection of the laws.

Congress passed the measure but then ran into a president who was opposed to their aims. Andrew Johnson, who took over as president after Abraham Lincoln was assassinated, was a Democrat from Tennessee. Although he had staunchly supported the Union against the Confederacy, he disliked the idea of granting sweeping civil rights to blacks and he proved a stubborn obstacle to legislative efforts to extend civil rights guarantees to blacks. Johnson vetoed the Civil Rights Act; however, Congress had the votes to override his veto and the measure was passed in late 1866.

The Fourteenth Amendment

Angered by Johnson's attitude and by the continuing stories of atrocities against blacks in the South, the Republican-controlled Congress took even more drastic steps to protect the rights of the freed slaves. They passed the Reconstruction Act of 1867 which temporarily took away local rule from the former Confederate states, unseated their elected congressional delegations, and divided them into five military districts administered by martial law. It required Southern states to adopt new constitutions that

Black men vote in an election during Reconstruction. The Civil Rights Act of 1866 declared former slaves to be citizens.

provided for the rights of blacks, including voting privileges. Federal troops were authorized to enforce the act and patrol polling places to insure that blacks were not denied the right to vote.

The Republican members of Congress feared that the new laws they had enacted for the protection of blacks would be repealed as soon as the former Confederate states were allowed to return their members to Congress. In order to prevent this, they decided to adopt the core of the Civil Rights Act of 1866 as the Fourteenth Amendment to the Constitution. The proposed amendment would prohibit the states from passing any legislation "which shall abridge the privilege or immunities of citizens of the United States, or shall deprive any person of life, liberty, or property without due process of law, or deny to any person within their jurisdiction the equal protection of the laws."[13]

Bucking vehement opposition from President Johnson, Congress swiftly voted to set the proposed amendment before the states for ratification. It put pressure on the Southern states by giving them a choice between approving the amendment and losing seats in Congress. Faced with the terms dictated by Congress, the former Confederate states, one by one, ratified the amendment and it became law in 1868.

Rays of Hope for Equality

By the end of 1868 the situation had quieted enough that military rule had been ended in all but three Southern states. But, still concerned that former Confederate states might at some point deny blacks the right to vote, Congress put forth another amendment proposal. The Fifteenth Amendment, which specifically guarantees blacks the right to vote, was adopted in 1870. Congress then, in a separate action, made it a federal crime to interfere with a person's right to vote. By blunting the worst outrages of the Black Codes, the adoption of the amendments, the Civil Rights Acts, and the use of federal troops to enforce the laws, ushered in a period when African Americans were able to vote in significant numbers. As a result, blacks won dozens of seats in state legislatures and captured many local government offices.

In the early 1870s it seemed possible that some form of accommodation of blacks' rights would be achieved in the South. Although aggressively racist groups were still harassing and terrorizing black citizens, a number of alternative points of view were being put forward. Most common of these was a widespread belief that blacks were inferior, but not to be hated or feared. Thus many people were not interested in degrading or humiliating blacks, nor did they necessarily believe in strict segregation between races. Their viewpoint was stated by Governor Thomas Jones of Alabama: "The Negro race is under us. He is in our power. We are his custodian. . . . We should extend to him, as far as possible, all the civil rights that will fit him to be a decent and self-respecting and law-abiding citizen." [14]

Quite different from this paternalistic approach was the political movement known as populism, which championed the cause of poor farmers. Many struggling white farmers found themselves in the same position as blacks. They had little voice in government and little influence on a society controlled largely by the wealthy. The strengthening of civil rights protections of blacks tended to benefit all the poor and working-class people. James W. Loewen notes, "The southern reconstruction legislatures started many needed and long overdue public improvements . . . strengthened public education . . . spread the tax

Black voters helped elect the first African American senator and representatives, pictured here.

burden more equitably . . . and introduced overdue reforms in local government and the judicial system."[15] As a result, there was a natural alliance between blacks and lower-income whites, even if some suspicion and prejudice remained. In addition to these views, there were small numbers of people, even in the South, who believed in total equality of the races.

For a brief time established political leaders in the South openly courted black voters, realizing that their support could spell the difference between victory and defeat. The variation in attitudes and interactions between blacks and whites was such that in the 1870s a fervent Northern abolitionist, Colonel Thomas Wentworth Higginson, was able to report that in his tour of the South he found that blacks were generally treated with a fair amount of tolerance and acceptance.

White Supremacists Fight Back

Throughout the Reconstruction period, however, the white supremacist forces were retrenching. They fought their battle against inclusion of blacks with four different strategies: economic pressure, legal maneuvers, societal exclusion, and violence. According to C. Vann Woodward, "The determination of the Negro's 'place' took shape gradually under the influence of economics, of political conflicts among divided white people, conflicts that were eventually resolved in part at the expense of the Negro."[16]

On the economic and political fronts, the upper classes of whites tried to sabotage the potential black-white alliance of poor farmers in the Populist movement by building on resentments and fears. Having been ruined economically by the Civil War, the Southern states faced a long, agonizing struggle to recover, no matter who was in charge. Impatience with the pace of the recovery was exploited to create the myth that the Southern governments of the Reconstruction era were dominated by uneducated, clueless blacks and had failed disastrously.

The myth of black irresponsibility, along with dislike of "carpetbaggers"—northern entrepreneurs who came south seeking personal gain at the expense of local residents, created a backlash against the racially open governments in power at the time. White supremacists further fanned the flames of resentment, urging poor whites to join with them against the Populist threats of racial mixing and loss of their lands and jobs to the newly freed blacks. Such arguments gradually turned poor whites against blacks and kept the Populist movement from building steam.

On the legislative front, Southern states avoided the kind of outright persecution of blacks that would invite retaliation from the North. Instead of prohibiting blacks from voting, they turned to subtle measures that would accomplish the same ends. The most effective of these actions was the creation of the poll tax, beginning in Georgia in 1871. The poll tax was a fee charged for the privilege of voting. On its face, such a tax was nondiscriminatory because every person was required to pay the same amount. But since virtually all blacks were poor, the tax effectively removed blacks from the voting process in many locations.

Socially, white supremacists found ways of keeping blacks down that were beyond the reach of the law. On the everyday level, clerks in stores and banks were told to serve white customers before blacks. Wherever they turned, blacks trying to work their way up economically found roadblocks in their paths, many of them worse than having to wait to be served. For example, vigilante groups continued a campaign of terror unchecked in many counties. In 1871 a powerful group of whites in South Carolina threatened black legislators with violence if they did not resign. In the following years such a campaign of murder and arson was launched against blacks and their supporters throughout the South that President Ulysses Grant expressed to South Carolina officials his indignation at acts which he described as "cruel, bloodthirsty, wanton, unprovoked," noting that they were "a repetition of the course that has been pursued in other states within the last few years."[17]

Last Federal Legislative Attempt

Congress made one last attempt to guarantee protection of Negro rights in 1875 by proposing new civil rights legislation. The Republicans wanted a firm declaration that outlawed dis-

President Ulysses S. Grant was appalled at the violent acts committed against blacks in the South and openly criticized the offenders.

crimination by race. However, Democrats and conservatives insisted that was going too far and would force whites to accept blacks as social equals. In the end, the Republicans saw that they no longer had the votes to impose their program and so they opted for a compromise. Rather than outlawing discrimination in its entirety, the Civil Rights Act of 1875 guaranteed all citizens, including blacks, equal protection under the law. Part of the act said, "All persons within the jurisdiction of the U.S. shall be entitled to the full and equal enjoyment of the accommodations, advantages, facilities, and privileges of inns, public conveyances

ELECTION MESS OF 1876

One of the most influential events in the history of the struggle for civil rights for blacks in the South was the presidential election of 1876. In the popular vote, Democrat Samuel Tilden of New York outpolled Republican Rutherford Hayes of Ohio, by roughly 264,000 votes. This gave Tilden 184 undisputed electoral votes, only one short of the number required for election, compared to 163 for Hayes. Twenty-two electoral votes, however, were disputed: those coming from Florida, Louisiana, South Carolina, and Oregon. The official returns favored the Democrats, giving Tilden the victory. But after widespread reports of fraud, intimidation, and violence against Republicans in the four states, federal election officials refused to accept the disputed votes.

By the end of President Andrew Johnson's term, the issue still had not been decided. In the end, Congress formed an electoral commission on January 29, 1877, composed of five members of the Senate, five from the House of Representatives, and five from the Supreme Court. The Senate and House members of the commission were evenly split between Democrats and Republicans. However, the Supreme Court justices included two Democrats, two staunch Republicans, and Justice Joseph Bradley, who was regarded as the most neutral of the remaining Republicans on the bench. Bradley, however, sided with the Republicans consistently, and all twenty-two disputed votes were awarded to Hayes, who then won the election by one electoral vote.

Angry Senate Democrats threatened to tie up the issue indefinitely, leaving the United States without a president for a dangerously long period of time. In intense negotiations, Democrats agreed to accept Hayes as president in exchange for a promise by the Republicans to remove all federal troops from the South.

on land or water, theaters, and other places of public amusement subject only to the limitations established by law, and applicable alike to citizens of every race and color."[18] As events would later prove, the law contained loopholes that segregationists could exploit, particularly in the area of private discrimination against blacks.

No sooner had the last federal troops departed from the South in 1879 than blacks began to see an erosion of the equal protection of the laws supposedly guaranteed to all citizens. At the same time, congressional representatives from the North became preoccupied with other matters and declined to accept further responsibility for the condition of blacks in the South.

More than half a century would pass before Congress made any further effort to protect the rights of black people. The era of Jim Crow—an official policy of segregation of races—was about to begin.

Chapter 2

Background of the *Plessy* Case

FOLLOWING THE DEPARTURE OF FEDERAL TROOPS from the South, the status of blacks in those states declined steadily as the white supremacists consolidated control and created a culture of enforced segregation. Southern governing bodies began passing laws that created, required, and enforced the separation of races.

The Separate Car Law that Homer Plessy challenged was just one of a wide network of discriminatory laws that became known as Jim Crow laws. Ironically, neither the term *Jim Crow* nor the idea of separate car laws were an invention of the South. Jim Crow was a somewhat derogatory term whites used in referring to blacks after it had been popularized by a white entertainer from Ohio. The first known Separate Car Law originated in 1841 in Massachusetts, one of the hotbeds of the abolitionist movement.

A New Social Dilemma

Public transportation became one of the major testing grounds for the new status of freed slaves in the South. In most social situations involving blacks and whites, tradition and custom had been well established. Some degree of separation between the races could be maintained fairly easily. It was generally accepted that blacks and whites did not live in the same neighborhoods, worship in the same churches, or attend the same schools. As long as this pattern was maintained, there were few conflicts.

Interactions between the races were most likely to occur in commerce. White proprietors of stores were often willing to accept blacks' business on the condition that the transactions were short and impersonal. Blacks could make purchases as long as they did so quietly, quickly, without challenging the prevailing understanding that they were second-class customers. However, areas of commerce in which long-term contact might occur were a different matter. Despite the clear language of the Fifteenth Amendment, most public establishments such as restaurants, inns, and recreational facilities did not serve blacks.

With respect to public transportation, however, several factors clouded the race relations issue. For example, public transportation had become widely available relatively recently, and there were few established social conventions that covered the new situation.

The first Separate Car Law was passed in Massachusetts (Boston pictured in 1840). This law required blacks and whites to travel in separate train cars.

This drawing depicts a passenger train car reserved for whites. After slavery was abolished, the South began to regulate public transportation along racial lines, prohibiting blacks from traveling with whites.

In addition, public transportation followed the lead of ocean liners which offered luxurious facilities for those who could pay the first-class fare, while the poor endured separate, far less comfortable accommodations. Passenger trains followed suit with a "smoking car," which for a reduced price offered uncushioned seats and tolerated behavior that was not acceptable among the more refined people of society. This policy of separation by charging different fares did not mesh neatly with the Southern practice of separation by race. Both blacks and whites who had the money and wished to ride in comfort could do so by paying first-class fare, while those of both races who could not afford first class were obliged to travel together in the smoking car.

As a final complication, public transportation often carried passengers long distances and could take them through various localities where the rules and traditions were different. What should happen, for instance, when a black passenger boarded a train in an area of the North where segregation was not customary and traveled into the South, or vice versa?

Early Transportation Racial Policies

Following the Civil War, Southern attempts to regulate public transportation along racial lines bore the harsh stamp of the Black Codes. In 1865 the Mississippi legislature made it illegal for "any freedman, negro, or mulatto, to ride in any first class passenger cars, set apart, or used by and for white persons."[19] The legislature did not require any special accommodation for black passengers and put no restrictions on whether blacks and whites could mix in the second-class cars. Florida and Texas were quick to pass similar laws.

In 1868 the Texas legislature became the first legal body to *require* separate accommodations for black and white passengers. The Separate Car Law it passed required all railroad companies operating within the state to include on all passenger trains a special car for recently freed black slaves. Despite the neutral wording of the Mississippi, Florida, and Texas laws, all three were regarded with suspicion by the state Reconstruction legislatures, and Reconstruction lawmakers promptly repealed these acts.

In the 1870s there was considerable discussion of the issue of separate transportation cars. While strict segregation of transportation cars, legal or not, was practiced in many areas, in other places there was more interest among the wealthier, more influential members of Southern society in separating themselves from coarse or offensive behavior than in strict black-white separation. According to some sources, well-dressed black passengers with refined manners came to be accepted as legitimate riders in first-class transportation. A Charleston newspaper editorial made the case that appearance and behavior were more important a consideration in travel than color, declaring, "To speak plainly, we need, as everybody knows, separate cars or apartments for rowdy or drunk white passengers far more than Jim Crow cars for colored passengers."[20]

The overall effect was that in 1879 an Englishman touring the South reported with surprise that "the humblest black rides

with the proudest white on terms of perfect equality and without the smallest symptom of malice or dislike on either side."[21]

Introducing Separate but Equal

Following the withdrawal of federal troops, however, and the
growing sentiment of municipalities toward Jim Crow segregation, states began taking a closer look at the public transportation
situation. The trains and streetcars began to stand out as a glaring contradiction to the accepted social structure of the South.
Nowhere else but on public transportation were blacks and
whites coexisting as if they were equals. As a result, public carriers increasingly became the target of new legislation.

At first the state governments tended to be cautious about
taking actions that might be seen as a revival of the Black Codes.
Those who were genuinely concerned with fairness toward what
they considered to be the inferior race found common ground
with white supremacists, who feared further controls on the
South might result from a refocusing of Northern concern for the
welfare of blacks. Therefore, when Southern lawmakers set
about designing laws to correct what they saw as an awkward
social problem aboard trains, they devised a way that did not, in

THE ORIGINS OF JIM CROW

A white singer and dancer, variously recorded in history as
Tom, Dan, or "Daddy" Rice, gained national fame in the early 1830s
for performing musical acts while blackening his face with burnt cork
and impersonating African Americans. One day while walking on a
street in Cincinnati, Ohio, Rice came across a small Negro boy who
was dancing and singing a song called "Jump, Jim Crow." Rice
copied the routine and included it in his act, acting the part of a character he called Jim Crow. This character began appearing in advertising for the show as early as 1832.

Rice's Jim Crow character was a highly stereotyped depiction, common at the time, of the happy, strutting, ignorant black man. The use
of the term *Jim Crow* for blacks spread quickly from this and various
other sources and the 1841 law requiring separate railway cars for
blacks in Massachusetts was commonly referred to as a Jim Crow law.
Eventually Jim Crow became identified with all racial segregation
laws and policies in the United States.

their opinion, openly degrade blacks. So it was that the "separate but equal" racial policies came into existence. Southern perspective was that a reasonable person would not object to whites desiring to remain socially distant from blacks so long as the blacks had facilities just as good as whites'.

In 1881 Tennessee became the first state to apply the separate but equal philosophy to public transportation. Its legislature enacted a law requiring public carriers to "furnish separate cars, or portions of cars cut off by partition wall, which all colored passengers who pay first class rates of fare may have the privilege to enter and occupy."[22] The legislature touted the law as generous concession to blacks. Indeed, many blacks initially welcomed this and other separate but equal laws. This attitude was the result of experience with ticket agents who refused to sell first-class coach tickets to blacks who wanted them and had the money to pay. Even in places where blacks were allowed first-class accommodations, they were sometimes yanked out of them and forced into smoking cars as soon as the train reached a more strongly segregationist area where the first-class coaches were strictly for whites. In many other areas of life, particularly in education, blacks had been forced to make do with vastly inferior facilities than those offered to whites. In view of these realities, the idea of equal facilities, even segregated ones, struck them as a great improvement over their present situation.

A few years after Tennessee introduced its separate but equal car law, Florida passed a similar law. It couched its language in terms that appeared to be even more considerate of blacks than Tennessee's law, saying that "no white person shall be permitted to ride in a negro car or to insult or annoy negroes in such car."[23] Mississippi, Texas, North Carolina, and South Carolina followed suit with similar separate but equal railroad laws.

But while the wording of such laws appeared to grant Negroes equality with whites, they could not remove from common knowledge the reason for the separation—namely, the prevailing opinion among whites that associating with black people was beneath their dignity. In effect then, these laws were key in reinforcing the power of whites in American society. Every separate but equal law was a public symbol of the domination of one race by another.

As these laws were being passed and put into place in the late 1880s, there developed a wide disparity in the degree of segregation from community to community. Many reports from that era insist that blacks commonly rode in compartments with whites. As late as 1890 a Richmond newspaper dismissed suggestions that the city segregate its streetcars with the claim, "We do not know of a city in the south in which discrimination is made on the street cars." [24] Yet reports from other Southern cities describe strict enforcement of separation in both travel and public accommodations.

Discrimination on the Rise

There was little opposition to this new wave of Jim Crow laws that swept the South in the late 1880s. The general feeling in the North was that the Civil War was now more than twenty years in the past, the slaves had been freed, and the North had done all they could do to ensure that they got a fair shake in the South. Now Southern blacks were on their own.

When Republican president Benjamin Harrison and other federal officials took no action regarding legislative infringements on blacks' rights, Southern leaders continued passing state and local laws that oppressed black

Representative Benjamin Arnett spoke out against laws that oppressed blacks.

people. Whites grew bolder in their discrimination, and refusal to serve blacks in public places became the rule throughout the South as early as the mid-1880s. In a speech delivered in 1886 Benjamin Arnett, a black clergyman elected to the Ohio state legislature, said, "I have traveled in this free country for twenty hours without anything to eat; not because I had no money to pay for it but because I was colored." [25]

But the most devastating rollback of black privileges came in the area of voting. There were two legal methods of depriving blacks of the vote that grew popular at the end of the 1880s. The first, introduced by white politicians in Mississippi in 1890, made the poll tax cumulative. Instead of paying a given amount at each election, a voter had to pay the same amount for every year in which he was eligible to vote but had not voted. Even those who worked hard to improve their economic position in hopes of saving enough to pay the poll tax for one election suddenly found themselves priced out of the voting booth for life. There was no question who was targeted by this policy, which was adopted as part of the new Mississippi constitution. Using the openly racist language of the day, Mississippi governor James K. Vardawn bragged, "The Mississippi constitutional convention of 1890 was held for no other purpose than to eliminate the nigger from politics." [26]

Literacy Tests for Voting

White segregationists, however, discovered a serious political problem with the poll tax: it prevented poor whites from voting as well as poor blacks. Fearful that disgruntled whites would join forces with blacks in the Populist movement, Southern segregationists hit upon the tactic of the literacy test. Pointing to the desirability of a well-informed voting public and insisting that the ability to read was crucial to carrying out this civic duty, they instituted the literacy test at the polls. Prospective voters had to prove to an election judge that they could read and understand the basic parts of the U.S. and state constitutions. Proponents of the literacy test claimed that the requirement was completely impartial; it would ban illiterate or poorly informed whites as well as blacks. In practice, however, the policy was designed to weed out only black voters. State laws gave election officials, all of whom were white, absolute authority to decide whether or not a prospective voter passed the literacy test. They were not required to give any reasons or supporting evidence for their decisions. As a result election officials could pass all white voters and reject black voters regardless of how individuals performed on the tests. Faced with this and other obstacles, blacks in many locations no longer even attempted to vote. Those who did increasingly risked violence and even death at the hands of violent racists such as the Ku Klux Klan.

White segregationists achieved their goal of eliminating blacks from the voting process. In Louisiana, for example, more than 130,000 blacks cast votes in elections during the early 1880s. That number dwindled to fewer than 5,000 in the last decade of the century. This in effect left blacks at the mercy of the white population who each year put the South more steadily in the grip of legally sanctioned segregation.

Opposition to the Separate Car Law

Well before the twentieth century, most blacks had realized that the separate but equal legislation was a recipe for disaster. Some believed that, given the obvious contempt of so many whites for black people, "separate but equal" would quickly and inevitably turn into "separate and unequal." Indeed, in many areas great emphasis was placed on the "separate" part while little attention was paid to the "equal." Famed black educator Booker T. Washington complained that "in every one of the Gulf states, the Negro is forced to ride in railroad coaches that are inferior in every way to those given the white, and they are made to pay the same fare as whites."[27] Washington was representative of blacks who did not oppose the separate but equal concept, but pushed for guarantees that the equal part would be honored.

Many other blacks, however, opposed the entire concept of separate but equal. They maintained that such laws and policies were being used to get around the law of the land. They saw

THE INVISIBLE EMPIRE

The Ku Klux Klan originated as a social club for Confederate war veterans. On December 24, 1865, a group of veterans gathered in a law office in Pulaski, Tennessee, and formed a group that they named the Ku Klux Klan after the Greek word *kuklid*, which means "circle." Part of the fun of the enterprise was maintaining secrecy and creating mysterious rituals that puzzled onlookers. Included among these rituals was the wearing of white robes and hoods. The idea of the Klan as an organization of Southern white comrades spread rapidly from state to state.

The organization took on a racist posture when Klan members observed the terrifying effect that their trademark white hoods and robes had upon some of their black neighbors, who believed in ghosts and other supernatural beings. Not all Ku Klux Klan cells were violent, but in many places the Klan became an organization of terror, intimidating African Americans and their sympathizers and committing acts of violence against them.

In the 1870s President Ulysses Grant and his administration were so incensed by the brutal deeds of Klan members that they had the organization outlawed and authorized the federal army to wage war against it. Although driven out of South Carolina and suppressed across the South, the Klan was never totally extinguished. As Jim Crow rule became firmly entrenched in the South, it revived, with a decidedly political slant. According to James W. Loewen in *Lies My Teacher Told Me*, "The new KKK quickly became a national phenomenon. It grew to dominate the Democratic Party in many Southern states, as well as in Indiana, Oklahoma, and Oregon." By 1920 the Klan's membership rolls had swelled to more than 2 million.

By World War II the Klan's activity had again diminished. It revived as a reaction to the civil rights movement of the 1950s and 1960s, then dwindled in the 1970s, as most Americans vigorously rejected its policy of terrorism and hate crimes. The Klan remains in existence today as a small group that promotes the cause of white supremacy.

---

every separate but equal segregation law as a clear statement that whites considered blacks an inferior race. Therefore, the separate but equal laws continued to promote racism.

Blacks had some nervous but reluctant allies in their opposition to the Separate Car Laws. The railroad companies, many of which were headquartered in the North, had a very practical reason for opposing such laws quite aside from racial beliefs: They cost them money and made it difficult to stay in business if instead of getting by with two passenger cars (one first-class and one smoking), they were now required to furnish four. On most of the lesser-traveled routes there was not enough passenger business to justify so many cars. This was particularly true of the blacks-only cars, as few blacks could afford to travel at all. Some of the railroad companies ignored the law in various areas where they believed they could get away with it. However, they dared not openly campaign against the Separate Car Laws, particularly in the South, for fear of alienating white passengers and stirring up hostilities.

The New Orleans Protest

In most of the South, blacks had little choice but to accept the indignity of the separate but equal laws. The whites' political power, wealth, and organization; the culture of the times; and widespread intimidation and violence against blacks combined to ensure the passage of segregationist laws over the protests of the outnumbered black legislators. New Orleans, Louisiana, was a rare exception to the rule of passive acceptance. It had a large Creole population, people of mixed black and French ancestry, dating back to the city's beginnings under French rule. These people had

The Ku Klux Klan terrorized blacks in the South and supported white supremacy.

Booker T. Washington accepted the separate but equal concept, but he felt that blacks were not receiving services on par with whites.

enjoyed freedoms and privileges not available to blacks in most areas of the South, and had founded the nation's first African American newspaper. New Orleans's French-speaking Black Creole community was incensed that the result of the Civil War seemed to be that they now enjoyed fewer rights than before the war.

When a separate car law was proposed in the Louisiana legislature in May 1890, some New Orleans blacks, such as former

Louisiana governor P.B.S. Pinchback, argued in favor of accepting the new law as a guarantee of first-class accommodations for black riders. They warned that blacks would only make things worse for themselves by stirring up trouble with the increasingly powerful white supremacists. But others, such as Randolphe Lucien Desdunes, scoffed at such fears. "It is more noble and dignified to fight, no matter what," he said, "than to show a passive attitude of resignation. Absolute submission augments the oppressor's power and creates doubts about the feelings of the oppressed. . . . Liberty is won by continued resistance to tyranny." [28]

Desdunes and sixteen others among the city's more prominent blacks argued strongly against the measure. Among their arguments was an appeal to the Fourteenth and Fifteenth Amendments' guarantee of equality under the law. They declared that the proposed separate car law was contrary to the basic American ideals expressed in the Declaration of Independence and the Constitution. These efforts were in vain, however. The State House easily passed the bill in 1890 and the Senate gave its stamp of approval shortly thereafter.

New Orleans's black community was not ready to give up without a fight, however. They realized that the odds were strongly against them and that the only effective weapon they could use was the federal legal system, which was charged with enforcing the U.S. Constitution. One of the most respected Black Creoles in the city, Louis A. Martinet, a lawyer, editor, and physician, wrote columns in the *New Orleans Crusader* newspaper drumming up support for a legal challenge to the Separate Car Law. Martinet and his friends were determined to create a test case to force the U.S. Supreme Court to make a ruling as to whether a state could require discrimination in travel accommodations.

A Committee Forms

On September 1, 1891, black opponents of the new law in New Orleans organized the Citizens' Committee to Test the Constitutionality of the Separate Car Law. They eventually raised three thousand dollars to finance their challenge, but that was not

THE BLACK CREOLES OF NEW ORLEANS

Black citizens of New Orleans enjoyed a status unknown to most African Americans in the South. New Orleans was established by the French and even up to the time of the Civil War it was known as more European than American. A large group known as the Gens de Couleur, French for "Free People of Color," had lived in the city for a long time and gained some influence. They included former slaves who had purchased their freedom, immigrants from Haiti who arrived during the turmoil of that country's slave revolts, and a group known as the Black Creoles. These were the children of extramarital unions between wealthy Frenchmen and attractive black women. Marriages between races were illegal; but the children of such couples were not treated as illegitimate, and they received privileges not available to mixed-raced children elsewhere in the South. They were often well educated and many were sent to European schools.

The Black Creoles of New Orleans still suffered discrimination. They were not allowed to vote, for example. But by 1850 they had accumulated a great deal of property within the city.

The Civil War actually changed the status of the Black Creoles for the worse. Whites came to regard them as no different than the newly freed slaves. Nonetheless in the 1870s, the Black Creoles still had enough influence in New Orleans society to challenge and defeat in court whites who violated the antidiscrimination laws. At the time of the Plessy challenge, they were one of the few groups of blacks in the South with the experience and organization to mount any kind of a court challenge to Jim Crow law.

nearly enough to afford the legal representation they would need for a long and costly court fight. Fortunately, Martinet found an important ally in Albion Tourgee. A prominent white attorney from New York who had served for a time as a federal judge in North Carolina, Tourgee was probably the nation's most well known advocate for the rights of black people. He had been following the Separate Car Laws closely, as well as Negro opposition to them, and had reported on the situation in his column in a Chicago newspaper. The citizens committee received a crucial boost when Tourgee agreed to take charge of the case without pay.

That left them with one more major hurdle—the need to hire a local attorney to shepherd the case through the early stages in municipal and state court. Because blacks had been held back by inferior education over the years, there were few black lawyers in the South, and even Martinet had no experience with the type of constitutional challenge that the group was now pursuing. Moreover, while the racial climate in New Orleans was better than in much of the South, segregation sentiment was still strong enough that few white lawyers would stick their necks out by taking up a case such as this. Eventually, the citizens committee found James C. Walker. Walker, a white man, provided competent legal representation while maintaining such a low profile that many New Orleans residents believed he had been arguing *against* Plessy in court.

Now all that the citizens' committee needed was a legal strategy and a test case.

Chapter 3

Louisiana's Separate Car Law Goes to Court

T HE CITIZENS COMMITTEE to Test the Constitutionality of the Separate Car Law knew that the legal system was a stickler for proper procedures. They had to carefully design a test case that would bring into court exactly the issues they wanted to address and not give judges the slightest excuse to get sidetracked.

Looking for a Test Case

In order to best demonstrate the absurdity of segregation laws, the committee wanted their designated violator of the segregated car law to be a mixed-race person so light-skinned that a casual observer would simply regard that person as white. At first they thought that a woman forced out of a car would gain more sympathy. But to avoid the possibility of introducing gender issues that would cloud the point, they looked for a respectable, law-abiding, well-mannered, light-skinned black man.

The members debated how best to arrange the violation of the law. Some of them wanted to have the person board the train in another state that did not require segregated cars so that he could be forced out of the car on reaching Louisiana. Creating such a disruptive scene would put the defenders of the law in a bad light. Unfortunately, all the surrounding states had recently enacted their own Separate Car Laws and

*Like these children, Homer Plessy was light skinned and often passed as
white. Plessy was chosen partially because his light skin color would help
show the absurdity of the law.*

so a person would have to go a long way to find a place in
which he could legally board an integrated coach. Then
somehow he would have to manage to ride illegally in the
white coach long before he reached Louisiana, otherwise his
arrest and court case would take place in some other state or
local court far from Louisiana. If he waited until the train
reached Louisiana before moving to a white coach, that would
defeat the purpose of boarding in a nonsegregated state to
begin with. In the end they chose to have their volunteer
board a train in Louisiana.

More than anything, they feared the violence that could
result if their scripted law violation got out of hand. Their test

person might find himself in grave physical danger, particularly if segregationists got wind of the plan. To avoid setting up their volunteer to be beaten and thrown off the train upon crossing into a state with a separate car law, the committee decided to alert the authorities well in advance to arrange the arrest. Again, however, they had to be careful not to let such information get into the wrong hands. The committee decided to approach senior railroad officials for help in setting up their law violation.

Again, the committee ran into a problem. Officials of the first railroad company Martinet contacted were not interested in arresting anyone. In fact, they admitted that they did not even enforce the segregated car law. Their policy was to post signs telling passengers which race belonged in which car and explained to passengers which coach they were assigned. But once that was done, they turned their backs and stayed out of the issue. A number of other railways had similar policies of nonenforcement or had no interest in getting involved in the proposed test case. As Martinet observed in frustration, "the railroads are not in favor of the separate car law, owing to the expense entailed, but they fear to array themselves against it."[29]

First Try

Finally Martinet found one company, the Louisville and Nashville Railroad, that was willing to help the committee challenge the law, as long as the company's involvement in the scheme was not publicized. In fact, they insisted that the committee make arrangements for a white passenger to lodge the complaint against the person who entered the wrong car.

In late February 1892 the committee found a volunteer to break the law and get the case into court. Daniel Desdunes, Randolphe Desdunes's twenty-one-year-old son, who was only one-eighth black by heritage, agreed to carry out the committee's plan. On February 24 he purchased a first-class ticket for a trip from New Orleans to Mobile, Alabama. When he boarded the train, officials directed him to the car for colored passengers. Desdunes refused to enter the designated car and instead headed for a seat in the whites-only car, whereupon a complaint was sworn out against him. Desdunes was now officially accused of violating the Separate Car Law; the case was open.

While the New Orleans group awaited their court hearing, they carefully plotted their arguments. Their lead lawyer, Tourgee, unable to come to New Orleans, offered long distance advice, particularly on the key issue of framing the argument. The committee members had debated whether they should attack the Separate Car Law as a violation of the Constitution's Fourteenth Amendment or of its Interstate Commerce clause. Tourgee recommended going the latter route because the power of the federal government to regulate commercial travel between states had been solidly established, and the federal government was more favorably inclined to their position than Southern state governments. On this matter the committee argued that all citizens had the right to travel freely throughout the country and that only Congress could make a law regarding such travel. But Tourgee also recommended that their arguments include the claim that the Louisiana law violated both the Thirteenth and Fourteenth Amendments to the Constitution to prepare the way for a possible Supreme Court appeal.

When the case came before Judge Robert Marr, attorney Walker filed pleas challenging the law and arguing that Louisiana officials had no authority to make travel conditions subject to race. In their filing the citizens' committee declared that the Separate Car Law "establishes an insidious distinction between Citizens of the United States based on race which is obnoxious to the final principle of national citizenship, abridges the privileges and immunities of Citizens of the United States and the rights secured by the 13th and 14th Amendments to the Federal Constitution."[30]

Bizarre Twist

The case took a bizarre twist in April 1892 when Judge Marr mysteriously vanished. While the authorities attempted to learn the whereabouts of the judge, the trial was put on hold. Before it could resume, the Louisiana Supreme Court handed down a decision that disrupted Desdunes's case. In the matter of *Abbot v. Hicks*, a conductor working for the Texas and Pacific Railway was charged with breaking the law by admitting a black passenger to a white car.

The lawyer for the conductor argued successfully that the law was invalid because it had allowed a state law to supersede the federal government's authority in matters of interstate commerce. On May 25 the Louisiana Supreme Court agreed that the Separate Car Act was unconstitutional on trains that traveled interstate, and dismissed the case.

A train crosses a bridge in the South. A case on interstate train laws had been dismissed before Plessy v. Ferguson *came to trial.*

LYNCHING: RACIST AMERICA'S
SHAMEFUL HERITAGE

The idea of vigilante justice, of people taking the law into their own hands with no regard for the legal system, has appeared for centuries in cultures throughout the world. The United States, however, adopted its own particularly cruel version of this known as lynching. The term appears to have received its name from Charles Lynch of Virginia, a patriot who was especially noted for summarily executing some who remained loyal to the British during the American Revolution.

Between the Revolutionary War and the Civil War, lynching was generally a fate reserved for suspected criminals. Blacks were not singled out: Most were slaves, and any punishment due for their actions was the responsibility of their owners. But following the Civil War, as the seeds of white racism spread throughout the South, lynching became more and more commonly used as a mob activity against blacks. Between 1882 and 1968 there were 4,743 lynching deaths, often by hanging, recorded in the United States; 3,446 of the victims were black. Between 1880 and 1920, published figures indicate an average of 2 blacks were lynched in the United States every week, and historians suspect hundreds of such deaths went unrecorded. Nowhere was lynching more commonly employed than in Mississippi, where 539 blacks and 42 whites were killed by mobs.

Lynching reached its peak in 1892, the year in which the New Orleans group challenged the Separate Car Law. At least 230 lynchings are known to have occurred that year, 161 of them involving blacks. Lynch mobs became increasingly sadistic, burning, torturing, and dismembering their victims before killing them. One of the most shocking cases involved three black businessmen who were killed by a Memphis mob, apparently out of resentment of their success. This so outraged a young black woman named Ida Wells Barnett that she began a long, dangerous campaign to eliminate lynching, an effort that only gradually produced results. As late as 1919 the nation witnessed 83 lynchings, 76 of the victims being black.

As a result of this ruling, Desdunes's case was also dismissed since he, too, had been traveling on a train bound for Alabama. While this was a victory of sorts, it did not address the racial discrimination issues that the committee had hoped to remedy and it left intact the legal requirement of separate cars on public transportation within the state. If the committee wanted to challenge that aspect of the law, they would have to start from scratch with a new case involving transportation within the state.

A mob lynches two black men in Indiana. Lynching was very common after the Civil War.

Second Try

Soon the committee had found a new volunteer, Homer Plessy, who was a friend of Randolphe Desdunes. On June 7 Plessy violated the Separate Car Law on an intrastate route and pleaded not guilty before Judge John Ferguson.

With the interstate commerce issue now settled, Plessy's lawyers focused their efforts strictly on the Constitution's guarantees of individual rights. They claimed that the Separate Car Law was a violation of Plessy's rights under both the Thirteenth Amendment, which abolished slavery, and the Fourteenth Amendment's guarantee of equal protection under the law. According to Plessy's legal team, these amendments made laws that treated people differently according to racial distinctions unconstitutional.

On November 18 Ferguson ruled against Plessy, who appealed to the higher Louisiana courts. In December the Louisiana Supreme Court sided with Ferguson in declaring that the Separate Car Law did not conflict with either the Thirteenth or Fourteenth Amendment. The ruling was not unexpected, particularly since the chief justice of the Louisiana Court, Francis Nichols, had signed the Separate Car Bill into law when he served as the state's governor. The committee members had, however, accomplished their first goal in getting a challenge to the law on the docket. As far as they were concerned, the early court decisions were just preliminaries to the real trial. Now, in appealing their case to the Supreme Court of the United States, they would force the justices to decide for the entire nation whether separate but equal segregation laws were constitutional.

Hoping for a Change of Political Climate

Had Plessy's lawyers pushed aggressively, the case likely would have been presented to the U.S. Supreme Court by late 1893 or early 1894. But Tourgee was concerned about the prevailing political and social climate. As he examined the history of rulings made by the sitting justices, he grew apprehensive. Only one of the justices, John Harlan, had ever openly come out in support of the position they were arguing. A delay in coming to trial, Tourgee believed, would allow for the possibility of retirements from the bench and replacements that would provide a more favorable hearing.

Tourgee also believed that the Supreme Court did not simply examine issues objectively. In his opinion, "The Court has always been the foe of liberty until forced to move by public opinion."[31] He was hoping to rally public opinion to put pressure on the Court but this was unlikely to happen in the early 1890s. An editorial in the *Christian Recorder* in 1892 stated, "It is evident that the white people of the South have no further use for the Negro. He is being treated worse now than at any other time since the surrender [of the South at the end of the Civil War in 1865]."[32]

According to historian James W. Loewen, "In politics, the white electorate had become so racist by 1892 that the Democratic candidate, Grover Cleveland, won the White House partly by tarring Republicans with their attempts to guarantee civil rights to African Americans."[33] In 1893, however, an economic

Racist cartoons like this were common following the Civil War, when fewer people championed equal rights for blacks.

panic turned many voters, including a substantial number of Democrats, against the Cleveland administration. Tourgee hoped that the times were ripe for Republican gains nationwide, and that some more reform-minded legislators and local officials would be elected. Such people might reawaken the United States to the issue of equality, in turn fostering an environment in which the Supreme Court would be inclined to rule favorably on a separate car law case.

Because of Tourgee's reluctance to push forward the trial at a time when the Supreme Court's docket was crowded anyway, *Plessy v. Ferguson* did not come before the nation's highest court until April 1896.

Scientific Racism

Unfortunately for Plessy, the passage of four years only changed the social and political environment for the worse. Unlike the years directly following the Civil War, blacks in 1896 had few defenders and even fewer advocates. Politically, the national Republican Party was not about to risk losing the White House again because of charges they were too cozy with the black population.

Furthermore, the North's former indignation had mainly been aimed at the inhumane institution of slavery and at the cruel treatment dictated by the Black Codes. But to many people of good will, the principle of separate but equal was neither unacceptable nor improper. In those days of blatant discrimination against blacks in matters of education, employment, and strict separation of the races, few whites had opportunities to see that blacks were not intellectually and morally inferior to whites. Most representations of blacks in advertising, in art forms, and in political debate depicted them as almost childlike buffoons. In recent years scientists had begun weighing in ever more strongly on the issue to the detriment of blacks. In August 1895 representatives of the American Association for the Advancement of Science came out with the statement that "each of the great races, each ethnic group has its own specific powers, and [all groups] were not equally endowed."[34] Edward D. Cope, a world-famous paleontologist from the University of Pennsylvania declared, "The highest race of man cannot afford to lose or even to compromise the advantage it has acquired by mingling its blood with the lowest."[35]

Although the opinions of people such as Cope were based on incomplete and distorted data, the claims of public figures widely regarded as objective and unbiased observers carried a great deal of weight. With the majority of American social and natural scientists who addressed the issue accepting differences in races as objective fact, many educated persons assumed that the debate over whether racial equality existed had been settled scientifically.

An article written in the *Protestant Episcopal Review* in 1896 is representative of the common view of the times that blacks were lesser humans:

> It is apparent to all educated and interested observers
> that our systems of instruction thus far have failed to

PLESSY'S HIGH-PROFILE LAWYER

Albion Winebar Tourgee was born on May 2, 1838, in Williamsfield, Ohio. After obtaining a degree from the University of Rochester, he fought in the Union army during the Civil War, where he was wounded and later captured by the Confederates. A lawyer by trade, Tourgee moved to Greensboro, North Carolina, after the war and attempted to use his legal skills to help in the transition from a slave society to one of freedom for all. Tourgee rose to the position of superior court judge in North Carolina in 1868 and served in that position until 1874.

He achieved national fame with his reports to the North on the political situation in the South, particularly his 1870 letter to the *New York Tribune.* In that letter Tourgee detailed and documented in graphic detail the grisly torture and violence employed by the Ku Klux Klan against those working for African American rights in the South. In 1875 he wrote a novel entitled *A Fools Errand,* which was based on his experiences in Greensboro and included many of his views on the situation in the South. This became a national bestseller and catapulted Tourgee to the forefront of the civil rights movement.

Tourgee left North Carolina in 1879 and spent most of his remaining years writing novels and articles and working for Negro rights. He was appointed U.S. consul to France in 1905 by the Theodore Roosevelt administration and died the same year.

---

implement in the negro a desire for higher and purer religion, to develop and strengthen his moral sense, to decrease his tendency toward crime, to increase his industrial or technical capacity in the years in which it is most needed, to impart high ideals of living and the dignity of honest labor, to teach the necessity for frugality, thrift, or industry . . . to root out his feelings of dependence, and to teach him self-help or to obviously strengthen his reason or train his judgment.[36]

In view of such prevailing opinions, Tourgee realized that he had his work cut out for him. Making a case that separate but equal application of the law was not a good idea would be especially difficult since the Supreme Court had not experienced the sort of transition for which he had hoped. Justice John Harlan was the only member of the Court who had consistently voted in favor of legislation protecting black rights. The two new justices who had come onto the Court since 1892 were Deward D. White from Louisiana, a man who had once served in the Confederate army, and Rufus Peckham of New York, who had immediately established himself as one of the Court's most conservative members. Melville W. Fuller, who had in 1860 served as the presidential campaign manager for Stephen Douglas in his run against Lincoln, had been chief justice since 1888. He could be expected to share somewhat the racial views of Douglas, who ran on a proslavery campaign.

All in all, Tourgee knew it would be a decidedly unsympathetic Supreme Court that would hear his case. He could only hope that the legal points he brought up would be persuasive.

The Arguments for Plessy

On April 13, 1896, lawyers for the two sides appeared before the Supreme Court to present arguments. Plessy caught a slight break when David Brewer, who had been expected to offer serious opposition, was unable to take part in the proceedings.

Tourgee carefully avoided any attempt to claim that passenger coaches on the train were better furnished and maintained for whites than were those for blacks. Whether or not this was true was irrelevant to his argument and he did not want the Court bogged down in this area. The key issue for the Plessy side was their belief that forced separation of the races was wrong by its very nature. As Tourgee told the Court, "The question is not as to the equality of the privilege enjoyed, but the right of the State to label one citizen as white and another as colored in the common enjoyment of a public highway."[37]

Tourgee argued that this was no trivial matter. "The object of such a law is simply to debase and distinguish against the inferior race . . . for the gratification and recognition of the sentiment of white supremacy and white supremacy of right and power."[38] He warned that if the nation's highest court upheld such a law, the floodgates would be opened for discriminatory legislation throughout the land that would make blacks little better than slaves.

Tourgee based his argument on the first two civil rights amendments. He claimed that the Thirteenth Amendment's ban on slavery was a ban on treatment of blacks as if they were less than human. The Fourteenth Amendment guarantees equal protection of the laws, and this included, he said, protection against public policies that singled out anyone for degrading treatment. Tourgee asked the justices to put themselves in the shoes of a black person seeking to travel by train. He asked them to imagine "what humiliation, what rage would then fill the judicial mind," [39] if they were treated as if they were not fit to associate with other humans.

Tourgee then asked the justices to consider the absurd consequences that could result if they supported Louisiana's law regulating people according to physical appearance. If the state declared the Separate Car Law to be constitutional, then it followed that it also be able to require redheaded people to ride in a separate car. Under that same logic, what would prevent the

The U.S. Supreme Court of 1894 is pictured. The future of the Jim Crow laws was left to these justices to decide.

state from forcing white people to paint their houses white and black people to paint theirs black? A state could legally divide up streets and sidewalks and reserve one side for blacks and another for whites. Did the Court really want to create a precedent for states to exert that kind of control over the rights of individuals?

The Arguments for Louisiana

Lawyers representing Ferguson and the state of Louisiana responded to Plessy's challenge with four main points. First, the state had a right to enact laws designed "to promote the comfort of passengers on railway trains." [40] The Separate Car Law, it said, was merely an effort to regulate, for the benefit of all, the procedures of train transportation in Louisiana. It was designed to prevent problems that could prove harmful to society if such regulation were left entirely to the whims and passions of each passenger riding the train. Second, the law did not deprive anyone of equal protection of the laws; on the contrary, it specifically required the railroads to furnish equal accommodations for both races. The Louisiana Supreme Court had found the Separate Car Law to be legal as long as the accommodations were equal for both parties, and no one had presented any evidence that they were not.

Third, such laws were well within the accepted range of legislation and custom not only in the South but in the entire country. All one needed to do was look at the most respected institutions of society such as the schools, churches, the armed forces, and the institution of marriage. On this issue, Southerners pointed out some glaring hypocrisies of the Northerners who demanded integration in the South. For even while the North was fighting a bloody Civil War that was largely over the issue of slavery, its own army units were rigidly segregated. The federal military remained segregated at the time of the *Plessy* hearing. Furthermore, the North was nearly as adamant as the South in opposing interracial marriage, and in fact localities in both sections of the country had laws banning it. It seemed to those in favor of the Separate Car Law that racial distinctions were woven into the very fabric of American life, that such distinctions were universally considered to be proper, and that the Louisiana law was in the same vein as the distinctions that were taken for granted everywhere.

Finally, Louisiana's lawyers argued that, under the Constitution, the federal government had no right to interfere with the legitimate powers of the state. As the legislation in question guaranteed equal facilities for both races, no constitutional rights were being violated and the federal government had no business telling a state how to regulate its intrastate train traffic.

When both sides had completed their arguments, the matter was left for eight justices, all white men, aged fifty-one to eighty, to decide. The fate of the Jim Crow laws rested in the hands of Chief Justice Melville Fuller and Justices John Harlan, Horace Gray, Stephen Field, Henry Brown, George Shiras, Deward White, and Rufus Peckham.

Chapter 4

The Supreme Court Decides

ONE OF THE MOST IMPORTANT CONSIDERATIONS for a judge in deciding cases is the matter of legal precedent, or what has been decided in previous, similar cases. It is difficult to maintain an orderly society if the rules are constantly changing and so all judges pay close attention to precedent to provide consistency to the nation's law. Above all, they do not want people to think that legal matters are decided purely according to the whims of those who happen to be wearing the black robes at the time. Supreme Court justices generally contradict previous decisions only when they believe they can show that a lower court has erred or that a state or federal law is unconstitutional.

In looking for clues as to how the Supreme Court under Melville Fuller would rule on *Plessy v. Ferguson*, legal experts studied the precedents set by the Supreme Court in previous cases involving the Thirteenth and Fourteenth Amendments, as well as the tendencies of this Court in similar cases. However, the Court had not been consistent in these decisions, so Plessy and his lawyers had no way to predict how the Court would rule in their case.

The *Slaughterhouse* Cases

Because of the importance of precedent, the earliest major rulings regarding the Fourteenth Amendment were especially significant. Perhaps the most frequently cited of these rulings was the Supreme Court decision in the *Slaughterhouse* cases, which were decided in 1873.

These were combined cases concerning a law passed by the Louisiana state legislature in 1869 which gave to a single company, the Crescent City Livestock Landing and Slaughterhouse Company, the exclusive right to slaughter cattle within the city limits of New Orleans. Rival butchers in the city filed suit against the state, charging that the law arbitrarily discriminated against them. They cited the Fourteenth Amendment, claiming that by making it impossible for them to earn their living as butchers in New Orleans, the state was violating the amendment's guarantee of equal protection. The state of Louisiana responded that the intent of the law was not to discriminate against anyone but simply to regulate an industry in a way that would ensure proper community health. Slaughterhouses were messy, smelly places and potential sources of diseases. Failure to regulate them in a highly populated area would lead to the creation of a public nuisance.

The U.S. Supreme Court upheld the Louisiana law. In explaining its reasoning it said that the equal protection clause of the Fourteenth Amendment applied only to state laws that discriminated against Negroes as a class. This acknowledgment that the purpose of the amendment was to prevent discrimination against African Americans would have given comfort to Plessy's team.

However, the Court defined the privileges the Fourteenth Amendment protected very narrowly: "the privileges and immunities of citizenship of the United States"[41] were said to be different from the privileges granted under state

Melville Fuller was chief justice of the U.S. Supreme Court at the time of Plessy. The case was tried under his control.

law. The Court declared that, with few exceptions, the Constitution gives the state the right to decide what is a proper privilege of state citizenship.

The Court did little to clarify exactly what was covered by the Fourteenth Amendment and the 5-4 vote demonstrated no clear consensus even among the justices regarding the meaning of the amendment. The ominous part of the ruling for *Plessy* was that it could easily be used to support the contention that the Fourteenth Amendment did not conflict with the Louisiana law affecting the rights of U.S. citizens traveling in the state.

U.S. v. Cruikshank

The most disturbing precedent from the Plessy standpoint was *U.S. v. Cruikshank*, a case decided in 1875. The case stemmed from a race riot in which whites massacred a crowd of African Americans (estimates range as high as 280 deaths) in Colfax

A black family removes the body of a man murdered at the Colfax Parish massacre. The Supreme Court threw out charges brought against sixteen white men involved in the murders.

Parish, Louisiana, on Easter Sunday in 1873. Federal prosecutors brought indictments against sixteen of the white assailants under the Civil Rights Enforcement Act of 1870, which outlawed conspiracy or actions with the "intent to injure, oppress, threaten, or intimidate any citizen, with intent to prevent or hinder his free exercise and enjoyment of any right or privilege granted or secured to him by the constitution of laws of the United States."[42]

In this case the Supreme Court threw out the indictments on the grounds that the prosecution had failed to prove specific intent by the defendants to deprive blacks of civil rights. The decision cited the *Slaughterhouse* ruling in declaring that the rights of citizens under state law differed from those under federal law.

The Court ruled in *Cruikshank* that the Fourteenth Amendment only "secures the individual from the arbitrary exercise of the powers of the government," and that the amendment "does not add anything to the rights which one citizen has under the Constitution against another."[43] In other words, while the government could not violate the civil rights of individuals, the Fourteenth Amendment did not protect individuals whose civil rights had been violated by other individuals. Although the Court conceded that the Thirteenth and Fifteenth Amendments allow federal action to remedy denial of individuals' rights, it said that the prosecution in this case had been too vague and general to prove that the defendants had acted on the basis of "race, color, or previous condition of servititude."[44]

In a ruling that was again bewildering to supporters of blacks' civil rights, the Court ruled that the prosecution "did not show that it was the intent of the defendants, by their conspiracy, to hinder or prevent the enjoyment of any right granted or secured by the Constitution."[45] If the Supreme Court did not consider the massacre of hundreds as preventing the black victims' enjoyment of any constitutional right, Plessy would be hard-pressed to convince them the prohibition against blacks riding in the same car with whites was an infringement of any legal right either.

U.S. v. Reese

In 1876 the case of *U.S. v. Reese* presented a clearer challenge to the intent of the Thirteenth, Fourteenth, and Fifteenth Amendments. Two Kentucky election officials had been prosecuted for refusing to count the vote of an African American resident, in violation of both the Civil Rights Enforcement Act of 1870, which guarantees voting rights to all citizens, and the Fifteenth Amendment.

In a major blow to supporters of Negro rights, the Court ruled in favor of the election officials and dismissed the case, allowing the defendants to avoid a hefty fine for their actions. In a very narrow interpretation of the law, the Court conceded that the Fifteenth Amendment prohibited the denial of the right to vote based on race, but that Congress had overstepped its bounds in setting up a penalty for obstructing the vote. According to the Constitution, said the Court, the federal government had no powers other than those specifically mentioned by the Constitution and in neither that document nor the amendment was it given the power to assess penalties in local elections. This decision baffled supporters of blacks' rights who wanted to know what use the Fifteenth Amendment was under the Court's interpretation. The Court's siding with the state on this issue was a severe blow to those wishing to protect voting rights of blacks, and a bad precedent for those advancing Plessy's case against Louisiana law.

The Civil Rights Cases of 1883

The cause of civil rights took another devastating hit in 1883 with a group of five court cases from Kansas, California, Missouri, New York, and Tennessee. The civil rights cases were argued in one hearing because they all dealt with the issue of racial discrimination by private individuals against blacks. Two of the cases involved the denial of sleeping accommodations, two concerned denial of entry to a theater, and one, which hit very close to home for the *Plessy* case, involved the refusal to allow a black woman entry to a ladies' car on a passenger train. In

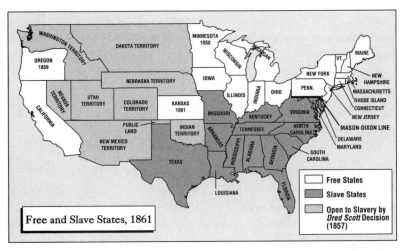

Free and Slave States, 1861

Free States

Slave States

Open to Slavery by *Dred Scott* Decision (1857)

all five cases, those refusing service were charged with violating the Civil Rights Act of 1875, which outlawed discrimination on the basis of race.

The majority of the justices ruled against the five discrimination victims because of their view that while the Fourteenth Amendment could prevent state-mandated discrimination, it did not allow states to infringe upon the private acts of citizens. The Fourteenth Amendment, said the Court, gave Congress no power to outlaw private acts of discrimination, only to forbid state laws that were discriminatory.

The refusal of the high court to apply constitutional protection to victims of private discrimination was a heartbreaking blow to civil rights advocates. It effectively gutted the entire Civil Rights Act of 1875 and made the federal government powerless in the face of racial discrimination by individuals. Nonetheless, Plessy's supporters could take some comfort from the ruling. Since the Court had at least affirmed that state discrimination was unconstitutional, the door was open to strike down Louisiana's Separate Car Law. Furthermore, Justice Harlan had presented himself as a bold champion of civil rights in his stinging dissent in this 1883 ruling. Harlan declared that the distinction between official state acts of discrimination and those done privately was "artificial." He pointed out that inns, amusement places, and transportation facilities were not private because they were licensed by government agencies and therefore subject to government control. Furthermore, he said that private acts of discrimination violated the Thirteenth Amendment because they inflicted "badges of slavery"[46] upon the victims. Reading this ruling, Plessy's supporters were certain they had at least one strong voice in the Supreme Court on their side.

The Jury Rights Cases

The Plessy side had further cause for optimism in two 1879 Supreme Court cases involving jury rights. In *Ex Parte State of Virginia*, Judge J.D. Coles of Pittsylvania County in Virginia was prosecuted for refusing to include African Americans in pools of jurors, in violation of the Fourteenth Amendment. In this case, the Court ruled against the argument that federal powers are too limited to allow them to take priority over state law. In announcing its decision, the Court wrote. "The prohibitions of the 14th amendment are directed to the States, and they are to a degree restrictive of state powers."[47] One sentence in the Court's ruling seemed to echo exactly the position that Plessy's lawyers had taken regarding the civil rights amendments. "One great purpose of these amendments," said the Court, "was to raise the colored race from that condition of inferiority and servitude in which most of them had stood, into perfect equality of civil rights within the jurisdiction of the United States."[48]

At nearly the same time, the Supreme Court issued a ruling in *Strauder v. West Virginia*. This case resulted from a suit brought by Taylor Strauder, a black West Virginian convicted of murder and sentenced to be hanged. Strauder argued that his Fourteenth Amendment rights had been violated because the state of West Virginia allowed only whites to serve as jurors, thereby creating a jury pool biased against him and depriving him of his right to equal protection under the law. The Supreme Court agreed, saying, "The 14th Amendment was designed to assure to a race recently emancipated, all the civil rights that under the law are enjoyed by white persons."[49] Regarding the right of a state to set its own laws regarding discrimination, the Court added that the amendment, "not only gave citizenship and the privileges of citizenship to persons of color but it denied to the State any power to withhold from them the equal protection of the laws."[50]

Most encouraging to civil rights supporters, the Court stated that the Fourteenth Amendment gave to blacks "the right to exemption from unfriendly legislation against them distinctly as colored; exemption from legal discrimination, implying inferiority in civil society, lessening the security of their enjoyment of the rights which others enjoy and discrimination which steps towards reducing them to the condition of a subject race."[51] Plessy's lawyers argued that separate but equal laws discriminating against blacks were exactly the kind of unfriendly legislation that this ruling outlawed. Supporters of the Separate Car Law, however, maintained that there was nothing in the separate but equal law that implied inferiority of the Negro.

Yick Wo v. Hopkins

One of the most fascinating court cases regarding the Fourteenth Amendment was *Yick Wo v. Hopkins*, decided in 1886. It involved racial discrimination, not against blacks but against Chinese. In the late 1860s many Chinese immigrants settled on the U.S. West Coast, and white government officials took steps to discourage them from taking up residency. One of the most blatant of these steps was an 1880 law enacted by the San Francisco board of supervisors that made it nearly impossible for those Chinese immigrants, who operated the vast majority of the city's laundry services, to stay in business. At issue was a new licensing requirement that was neutrally worded but had a clearly discriminatory purpose. Its effect was discriminatory as well: All but one of the 240 Chinese who applied were rejected while every white person who applied for the same license was accepted.

Yick Wo, who had been in the laundry business for twenty-two years, was one of those denied a license, but he continued to operate his laundry. This defiance netted him an arrest, and at his trial he was convicted. He appealed to the

San Francisco's Chinatown made news when Yick Wo, a Chinese launderer, won a case over racial discrimination. Plessy supporters hoped for a similar result.

California Supreme Court, which ruled against him, and then to the U.S. Supreme Court, where the justices ruled 9-0 in his favor.

The Court declared its disgust with what it described as the "naked and arbitrary power" of the city government. "The very idea that one man may be compelled to hold his life; or the means of living, or any material right essential to the enjoyment of life, at the mere will of another seems to be intolerable in any country where freedom prevails, as being the essence of slavery,"[52] said Justice Stanley Matthews, writing for the Court.

The Court's ruling stood in Plessy's favor in two ways. First, it declared that the Fourteenth Amendment really could restrict the power of state and local governments. Even more intriguing, the case showed how a law that showed no trace of discriminatory purpose had been used in a way that denies the equal protection of the laws. That was exactly Tourgee's argument against the Separate Car Law.

An Inflexible, Reluctant Court

Both sides, then, could point to Supreme Court precedents that would support their arguments. In trying to predict what the Court would decide, there were two other factors to consider. First, with the exception of Harlan, the justices were not particularly bold in their approach to the law. They generally kept a low profile and had a dim view toward dissents, which they considered showing off. They were far more comfortable when the entire Court was in agreement and worked hard to avoid split decisions. Secondly, in most of the cases that had come before them in recent years, the Court had generally taken a hands-off position regarding state laws.

The Court had a reputation for being inflexible rather than imaginative and showed a strong suspicion of any expansion of government power. As a general rule, the Supreme Court in recent years had interpreted the Constitution very narrowly and had tended to give states the benefit of the doubt over the federal government in most matters.

A Seven to One Vote Against Plessy

On May 18, 1896, the Supreme Court announced its decision. The justices dealt a crushing blow to Plessy and his supporters, voting 7-1 against their suit. Only the fiery nonconformist Justice Harlan had sided with their arguments.

The opinion explaining the ruling was written by Justice Henry Brown, a man considered to be among the more moderate members of the Court and one who was highly interested in achieving consensus among the group. He began by using the opinions in the *Slaughterhouse* and civil rights cases to dismiss *Plessy*'s claim that the Separate Car Law violated the Thirteenth Amendment. Taking a strict, literal view of the amendment. Brown wrote that it was "too clear for argument"[53] that a law regulating where people could sit on a railroad car had nothing to do with slavery even if it did discriminate.

The question then turned to whether the Louisiana law violated Plessy's right to equal protection of the law. Brown conceded that the intent of the Fourteenth Amendment was to establish absolute equality of the races before the law but denied any implication that blacks and whites had to be treated as if they were the same. Being actively involved himself in the American Society for the Advancement of Science, Brown firmly believed the inequality of the races was an established fact. "In the nature of things," he wrote, "[the amendment] could not have been intended to abolish distinctions based upon color, or to enforce social, as distinguished from political, equality or a commingling of the two races unsatisfactory to each other."[54]

Is the Louisiana Law Reasonable?

If that was the case, then the key issue was whether the separate but equal provisions of the Separate Car Law granted the equal protection of the law in accordance with the Fourteenth Amendment. Plessy's lawyers had not claimed that the facilities were unequal so the law was not being challenged on that basis.

Thus Brown was left with only one issue to decide: whether the mere fact of requiring a division of the passengers by race violated the equal protection clause of the Fourteenth Amendment. Brown could have cited *Yick Wo* in support of an opinion that such division by race has the potential for terrible abuse, and ruled against the law. But the core of Brown's argument was that the Court could make a "distinction between laws interfering with the political equality of the Negro and those that require the separation of the two races."[55] He noted that the Supreme Court, in its decisions in the *Slaughterhouse* cases and *Yick Wo v. Hopkins* prohibited only the "hostile legislation of the states."[56] Instead of citing *Yick Wo* to argue against racial discrimination, as Plessy's lawyers had hoped, he cited it in support of the Separate Car Law because the 1886 decision had disallowed discrimination that was unreasonable without addressing the issue of discrimination on the basis of race.

In support of this argument, he noted that there were many state laws that discriminated along racial lines which "have been generally, if not universally recognized as within the competence of the state legislature."[57] As an example, he cited the outlawing

THE MAN WHO WROTE THE *PLESSY* DECISION

It is one of the many ironies of the *Plessy* case that the man who wrote the opinion sanctioning state-sponsored segregation hailed from the strongly abolitionist state of Massachusetts. Henry Billings Brown was born on March 2, 1836, in South Lee, Massachusetts, where his father was a prosperous manufacturer. After attending the finest schools in the state, Brown eventually moved to Michigan where he practiced law and gained interest in politics. He failed in his attempt to win a seat in Congress in 1872 but was appointed to a federal judgeship by Ulysses Grant in 1875. A civic-minded man, Brown was thrilled with the chance to rule from the bench, saying that it allowed him, according to author Timothy L. Hall, "to exchange a position where one's main ambition is to win for one where one's sole ambition is to do justice."

As a Supreme Court justice, Brown could be somewhat unpredictable in his voting but seldom ventured into controversy. Although he had surprised observers by issuing a dissent in the Court's decision that a federal income tax law was unconstitutional, for the most part Brown was a consensus builder and perhaps the most moderate member of the Supreme Court in 1896. As such he was a natural choice to write an opinion on a case with potentially heated emotional overtones. Yet he failed utterly to fashion a convincing statement of the Court's position.

Brown has drawn the wrath of legal scholars and historians for his *Plessy* decision. In his defense, most historians concede that he was a product of his times who was merely stating the mainstream position of most Americans. In *The Plessy Case: A Legal-Historical Interpretation*, historian Charles A. Lofgren concludes that Brown "was a better justice than his opinion in Plessy suggested, but his judicial performance in this case has tended to overshadow his other modest accomplishments."

Supreme Court justice Henry Billings Brown wrote the opinion explaining the Plessy *ruling.*

THE RACIST LEGACY

As shocking as the statements made and conclusions reached by Brown and his colleagues in *Plessy v. Ferguson* may seem to Americans today, they reflect the views held by a great many Americans until well into the twentieth century. Throughout U.S. history, prominent Americans who are regarded as champions of liberty held views that cannot be classifed as anything but racist today. Thomas Jefferson, the man who wrote so elequently in the Declaration of Independence about all men being created equal, owned hundreds of slaves during his long life. Some of his writings indicate that he believed blacks to be inferior and that he supported expansion of slavery into the western states.

Even Abraham Lincoln, the author of the Emancipation Proclamation, who was convinced that slavery was evil, shared the racist biases of many of his contemporaries early in his political career. James W. Loewen, in *Lies My Teacher Told Me*, quotes Lincoln as responding to his debating opponent, Stephen A. Douglas, "I am not, nor ever have been in favor of bringing about the social and political equality of the white and black races—that I am not nor ever have been in favor of making voters or jurors out of Negroes."

Loewen notes that although another U.S. president, Woodrow Wilson, is primarily known as a man of peace who worked hard for the creation of the League of Nations, historians know him in another light:

> A southerner, Wilson had been president of Princeton, the only major northern university that refused to admit blacks. He was an outspoken white supremicist—his wife was even worse— and told "darky" stories in cabinet meetings. . . . Wilson personally vetoed a clause on racial equality in the Covenant of the League of Nations. . . . Wilson's legacy was extensive: he effectively closed the Democratic party to African Americans for another two decades, and parts of the federal government remained segregated into the 1950s and beyond.

of interracial marriages, a ban, he noted, that the vast majority of Americans believed to be reasonable. In addition, he pointed out that separate educational facilities for blacks and whites were a matter of law, not only in the South but in other areas of the country. Brown specifically cited the case of *Roberts v. City of Boston, Massachusetts,* in which the city's legally enforced separation of the races in public schools had been upheld by the state courts. This, said Brown, was considered reasonable discrimination. "A law," he concluded, "which merely implies a legal distinction between white and colored races has no tendency to destroy the legal equality of the two races."[58]

But was the discrimination in the Louisiana law reasonable? "We cannot say," wrote Brown, "that a law which authorizes or even requires the separation of the two races in public conveyances is unreasonable."[59] Nor did Brown see in the law any intent to injure or offend blacks. The law, he wrote, was enacted "in good faith for the promotion of the public good."[60]

Brown's opinion up to this point had been damaging enough to the cause of black civil rights. But then he went on to say that he saw no reason why any reasonable person could object to the law. "We consider the underlying fallacy of the plaintiff's argument to consist in the assumption that the enforced separation of the two races stamps the colored race with a badge of inferiority," he wrote. "If this be so, it is not by reason of anything found in the act, but solely because the colored race chooses to put that construction on it." Brown summed up his view of the racial situation in the land by writing, "If one race be inferior to the other socially, the constitution of the United States cannot put them upon the same plane."[61]

With that statement, endorsed by all but one of his colleagues, Henry Brown, in effect, declared state-required segregation to be legal in the United States.

Chapter 5

Plessy v. Ferguson:
Reaction and Legacy

THE SUPREME COURT'S DECISION AGAINST PLESSY was coun-
tered by a bold and passionate dissent by Justice John Harlan. This was not surprising since Tourgee had patterned many of
his arguments after Harlan's words in his dissents on previous
Fourteenth Amendment cases. But in *Plessy*, the eloquence of the
aging former slaveholder from Kentucky was particularly striking.

Harlan Attacks the Decision

Harlan attacked the majority's decision from many angles.
Despite Brown's assertion that the plaintiff's claim did not even
merit discussion, Harlan believed that Louisiana's Separate Car
Law *did* violate the Thirteenth Amendment. That amendment,
said Harlan, did more than outlaw the institution of slavery; it
also "prevented the imposition of any burdens or disabilities that
constitute badges of slavery or servitude." [62] Harlan reminded his
fellow judges that previous Supreme Court rulings had established that the railways were public highways; they were not the
private domain of a few privileged people. In Harlan's opinion, a
law that "regulates the use of a public highway by citizens of the
United States solely based on race" qualified as stamping a
"badge of servitude" [63] on the black race.

Harlan saw the Fourteenth Amendment as providing an
even stronger reason to rule the Separate Car Law unconstitutional. The other judges seemed to him to be trying to get
around the implications of a constitutional amendment they

76

found worrisome but which Harlan declared "added greatly to the dignity and glory" of the nation. It guaranteed the rights of all citizens to the rights and privileges of citizenship, including the use of public highways. "If a white man and a black man choose to occupy the same public conveyance on a public highway, it is their right to do so," said Harlan, "and no government, proceeding alone on the grounds of race, can prevent it without infringing the personal liberty of each." [64]

Harlan had nothing but scorn for Justice Brown's attempt to treat the Separate Car Law as a totally neutral way of separating

Supreme Court justice John Harlan was the only justice to agree with Plessy that the Separate Car Law was unconstitutional.

citizens for the comfort and convenience of each race, which blacks were wrong to view as an insult. Stripping away all pretense, Harlan wrote,

> Everyone knows that the statute in question had its origin in the purpose, not so much to exclude white persons from railroad cars occupied by blacks, as to exclude colored people from coaches occupied by or assigned to white persons. . . . The thing was, under the guise of giving equal accommodations for whites and blacks, to compel the latter to keep to themselves while traveling in railroad passenger cars.[65]

The Dissent Picks Up Steam

Harlan took Brown to task for a faulty and misleading analysis of precedents. He noted that many of the precedents Brown had cited were invalid because those rulings were made before the Fourteenth Amendment was passed. In fact, one of the purposes of the Fourteenth Amendment was to change the Constitution so that those old precedents no longer applied.

As for Brown's claim that laws requiring discrimination were perfectly legal as long as they were "reasonable," Harlan objected strongly that such a view had no basis in law. "Legislation either falls within the legislature's proper sphere or it does not. It if does not, its policy advantages will not save it."[66] In other words, if discrimination was prohibited by the Fourteenth Amendment, it did not matter how "reasonable" legislation mandating discrimination seemed to be. It was prohibited, period. As for "reasonableness," Harlan endorsed Tourgee's argument that the Separate Car Law carried to its logical extremes could spawn legislation that required blacks and whites to walk on separate sidewalks, to drive on different streets, even to sit on different sides of a courtroom. A state might even require Roman Catholics to sit in different railroad cars from Protestants. In short, the Separate Car Law was about as unreasonable as a law could get.

Justice Harlan was not immune to racial prejudice. In his opinion, he wrote, "The white race deems itself to be the dominant race in this country. So, I doubt not, it will continue to be for all time." [67] Yet in Harlan's understanding of his responsibility as a judge, his personal opinion of the races had no place in the law. In his most memorable phrase, he wrote that in matters of law, "Our Constitution is colorblind and neither knows nor tolerates classes among its citizens." [68]

Harlan saw the Court's ruling in support of separate but equal law as so flawed and so disastrous that he predicted it would do more damage than the notorious *Dred Scott* case. In a remarkable rebuke to his colleagues, he wrote, "The thin disguise of equal accommodations for passengers in railroad coaches will not mislead anyone, nor atone for the wrong this day done." [69]

Immediate Impact

Harlan, however, appeared to be a lonely voice crying in the wilderness, unheeded by anyone. Perhaps the Supreme Court's decision reflected the prevailing opinion in the country, or perhaps the white majority had lost interest in the post–Civil War fight for black civil rights. The decision provoked no outcries of indignation nor mass rallies of protest as the *Dred Scott* decision had sparked some forty years earlier. The nation's press let the decision pass virtually without comment.

On its most practical level, the decision meant two things: first, that Homer Plessy had to pay the fine specified by the Separate Car Law. In January 1897 he entered a formal guilty plea in a New Orleans courtroom to the charge of occupying the car reserved for whites, and handed over the twenty-five dollars. His moment in the public spotlight now over, Plessy faded from public view. He died in 1925.

Secondly, Louisiana's Separate Car Law was firmly in place and not subject to further challenge. The citizens' committee that had put Plessy up to the court challenge, aware all along of the odds against their fight, accepted the ruling with their heads held high. "In defending the cause of liberty," declared the committee, "we met with defeat but not ignominy." [70] The case itself was generally forgotten by the public and ignored even by historians.

Jim Crow as the Law of the Land

While *Plessy v. Ferguson* disappeared from public view, how-ever, the ruling added momentum to the growing official poli-cies of racial discrimination in the South. In fact, an Alabama government official at the time of the ruling declared that in matters of racial discrimination "we now have the sympathy of thoughtful men in the North to an extent that never existed before."[71]

This momentum is clearly demonstrated by the Supreme Court's ruling, two years later in a Mississippi voting rights case. In *Williams v. Mississippi*, the U.S. Supreme Court handed white supremacists another major victory when it upheld a poll tax and literacy requirement that in practice were applied only to blacks. According to the Court, the actual wording of the laws applied equally to blacks and whites, made no specific mention of an intent to discriminate against blacks, and therefore was not unconstitutional.

In effect the Supreme Court ruling gave official federal approval to the tactic of using the law to deprive black citizens of their right to vote. Realizing the possibilities that had opened for them, during the last decade of the nineteenth century every Southern and border state found ways to exclude the great majority of blacks from their elections. With their voting privi-leges abridged or denied, Southern blacks became powerless politically.

In the South, the Democratic Party built itself into an apparently unshakable bastion of white supremacy. From the time of the Civil War to the time of the *Plessy* decision, no Democrat in Congress, whether representing the North or the South, had ever voted in favor of a single piece of civil rights legislation. With black voters now out of the picture, the Demo-cratic Party held a virtual monopoly on all elective government positions in the region well into the middle of the twentieth century. In those states of the Union, the government was able not only to make racial discrimination legal but to require dis-criminatory practices be enforced as a matter of law.

RESTRICTING THE VOTE

Americans have long struggled with the issue of who is qualified to vote in a public election. During the nation's formative years, there were many who thought that only landowners should have the right to vote. Women were not allowed to vote until the twentieth century and as late as 1855, only five states in the Union allowed blacks to vote.

The Fifteenth Amendment was designed to eliminate the practice of denying people the right to vote based on race. But white supremacists found many ways to get around that amendment. Measures such as poll taxes and literacy tests made it difficult if not impossible for many poor whites as well as blacks to vote. In order to stem resentment and get poor whites on their side, white officials created the "grandfather clause."

A section of the Louisiana constitution passed in 1898, quoted in Walter L. Fleming's *Reading the Fine Print: Grandfather Clause in Louisiana*, provides an example of a grandfather clause:

> No male person who was on January first, 1867, or at any date prior to thereto, entitle to vote under the Constitution of statutes of any State of the United States, wherein he then resided, and no son or grandson of any such person not less than 21 years of age at the date of the adoption of this Constitution . . . shall be denied the right to register and vote in this State by reason of failure to possess the educational or property qualifications prescribed by this Constitution.

Basically, the grandfather clause allowed men to vote regardless of any other qualification if they had voted in 1867 or were descended from someone who voted in 1867. Since only whites had been allowed to vote in the South in 1867, the only purpose of the clause was to let poor whites get around the rules created to keep blacks from voting. It worked well, immediately reducing the number of black voters in the nation by one-third.

The grandfather clause was so blatantly unfair that the U.S. Supreme Court, which had seldom interfered with whites' attempts to control blacks in the past decades, declared such clauses unconstitutional.

A Pillar of Support for the Old Ways

Socially, life became increasingly burdensome for blacks, as white governments sanctioned the old methods of discrimination and imposed new ones. Slowly at first, but with increasing frequency over several decades, *Plessy* was cited by judges in support of Jim Crow laws.

Virtually every facet of life in the South was segregated. Blacks could not drink out of the same fountains, use the same public bathrooms, or play in the same parks as whites. They could not eat in most restaurants or stay in most hotels or inns. In 1899 the Supreme Court expanded its endorsement of the separate but equal laws to specifically cover public schools. Even Justice Harlan seemed to be swept away by the tide of public opinion that favored or at least tolerated segregation. Harlan, who had written so eloquently in favor of equal treatment of the races in *Plessy v. Ferguson*, wrote an opinion in this case in which he condoned racially segregated schools. After that, black schools, seldom adequate even during Reconstruction, were invariably inferior, with few textbooks or others resources; and blacks were denied access to public universities, medical schools, and law schools.

Segregation moved from separate coaches on cross-country trains to separate seats on city buses; blacks were forced to sit in the back. A Birmingham, Alabama, law even made it illegal for blacks and whites to play games such as checkers and dominoes together. Not only were the vast majority of churches strictly segregated despite preaching a doctrine of love for all humanity, but white supremacists invoked their most fervent religious beliefs in support of their actions. Theodore Bilbo, who served both as governor and U.S. senator from Mississippi, declared, "We the people of the South must draw the color line tighter and tighter. . . . The white race is the custodian of the Gospel of Jesus Christ." [72]

At first the decision in *Plessy v. Ferguson* was seldom invoked by white supremacists. But when legal challenges to these blatant denials of human rights were offered in the twentieth century, they discovered that the *Plessy* ruling was a powerful precedent in defense of their cause. Over several decades, *Plessy* was cited in dozens of court cases in support of Jim Crow laws.

Along with such deeply entrenched values, the force of the *Plessy* decision kept the South tightly in the grip of Jim Crow rule for more than a half century. But the South was not the only place where such discrimination was officially sanctioned. Prior to World War II, the U.S. Marine Corps refused to accept blacks

Black schools were typically inferior to white schools. Nearly every aspect of life in the South was segregated, including education.

even as low ranking messengers. During that war, segregated black military units were formed only over the objections of top officers and were seldom allowed to see combat.

The Dixiecrats

Following the war, President Harry Truman decided that forced segregation of the armed forces was not right. On July 26, 1948, he issued an executive order which said, "It is hereby declared to be the policy of the President that there shall be equality of treatment and opportunity for all persons in the armed forces."[73] This and similar stands in favor of racial integration by Northern Democrats so angered whites in the South that they turned away from Truman even though he was their party's highest elected official. Democratic delegates from Southern states gathered at their own states rights convention in 1948 and nominated Strom Thurmond of South Carolina as their presidential candidate.

African American marines aboard a U.S. Coast Guard transport during World War II. President Truman mandated equality in the armed forces.

Thurmond made it clear that his main issue was keeping blacks in their place. In a speech to the convention, Thurmond said, "I want to tell you that there's not enough troops in the Army to force the Southern people to break down segregation and admit the Negro race into our theaters, into our swimming pools, into our homes, and into our churches."[74] Thurmond's views were so popular in the South that he won four states and nearly caused Truman to lose the election to Republican Thomas Dewey.

Brown v. Board of Education

The separate but equal policy endorsed by *Plessy v. Ferguson* remained the law of the land for more than half a century. No Supreme Court ruling during that time made any attempt to modify or correct it. Typical of the Court's acceptance of the *Plessy* precedent was the opinion issued by Chief Justice William Howard Taft in 1927. Dismissing a case that challenged the con-stitutionality of segregated schools, Taft wrote that the issue "has many times been decided [by the Supreme Court] to be within

THE ISSUE THAT REFUSES TO DIE

Mississippi senator Trent Lott had just become the most powerful person in the U.S. Senate. The Republicans' victory in the 2002 elections had given him the job of senate majority leader. A month after claiming this heady victory, Lott attended the party celebrating retiring South Carolina senator Strom Thurmond's one hundredth birthday. During the festivities, Lott reminisced about Thurmond's run for president as the Dixiecrat candidate in 1948. As quoted by Evan Thomas in "Race to the Exit," *Newsweek*, January 6, 2003, Lott noted that he was proud that his state of Mississippi had voted for Thurmond and declared that had the rest of the country followed Mississippi's example, "we wouldn't have had all these problems over all these years."

Thurmond's only real campaign issue in 1948 had been segregation and Lott's public support of that candidacy touched off a storm of criticism. Republicans were put on the defensive by Lott's remarks, which reminded people that, contrary to their beginnings as the party of Abraham Lincoln, the Republicans have more recently been seen as unsympathetic to minorities.

Not wishing to encourage a perception that all its white members were segregationists, Republicans reacted swiftly to Lott's remarks. Despite Lott's apologies and pleadings that the comments had been careless and did not reflect his true views, the Republican leadership forced Lott to step down as majority leader. His fall from power demonstrated that, more than a century after the *Plessy* decision had been rendered, its effects were still driving U.S. politics.

Senate majority leader Trent Lott was forced to resign after he made segregationist remarks.

the power of the state legislatures to settle without the interven-
tion of the federal courts."[75] A civil rights worker's only weapon
against racism during this period was moral persuasion and that
was not enough to combat the entrenched forces of segregation.

*Thurgood Marshall became the first African American Supreme Court justice
when he was appointed in 1967.*

Change did not come until 1954, when the Court was asked to rule on an appeal filed by Oliver Brown and twelve other plaintiffs from Topeka, Kansas, claiming that the city's policy of separate but equal educational facilities discriminated against their young children in violation of the Fourteenth Amendment. In a key strategic move, Brown's lawyers did not argue that the facilities at the black school were inferior to those of the white schools. Had they won on that basis, they would only have forced Topeka to upgrade the black schools to the level of the white schools. Instead their lead lawyer, Thurgood Marshall, made a direct attack on racial segregation and the ruling of *Plessy v. Ferguson* by arguing that separate but equal policy inherently discriminated against blacks. By its refusal to allow blacks to mix with whites, the policy proclaimed whites to be superior, argued Marshall. He cited reports of psychologists to show the damage to black children's self-esteem and learning caused by such a policy.

On May 17, 1954, the Supreme Court unanimously ruled in favor of the Kansas plaintiffs and so at last overturned the decision in *Plessy v. Ferguson*. Writing for the Court, Chief Justice Earl Warren said, "Segregation of white and colored children in public schools had a detrimental effect upon the colored child. The impact is greater when it has the sanction of law. We conclude that in the field of public education the doctrine of separate but equal has no place."[76]

The Civil Rights Movement

The Supreme Court's ruling in *Brown v. Board of Education* did not immediately dismantle Jim Crow regulation in the South. More than one hundred members of Congress criticized the Court for its decision and few affected localities made any move to comply. A great struggle for civil rights ensued in the South. When black citizens of Montgomery, Alabama, under the leadership of Martin Luther King Jr., boycotted buses in 1955, in protest of their discriminatory policies, white citizens reacted angrily. Senator James O. Eastland of Mississippi displayed white racism at its worst when he addressed a rally of more than ten thousand whites gathered in opposition to the boycott in the Montgomery Coliseum. With a shocking parody of the Declaration of Independence that began, "When in the course of human events it becomes necessary to abolish the Negro race,"[77] Eastland drew applause from his audience and condemnation from much of the rest of the country.

During the civil rights movement, many blacks as well as white civil rights workers were attacked and beaten, even killed, for trying to dismantle the legal barriers to racial equality. Their courageous, nonviolent stand, however, eventually made a deep impression on people across the country. By 1965 the political and social climate had changed enough to allow passage of the 1965 Voting Act that returned to blacks the right to vote. By the early 1970s virtually all Jim Crow segregation laws had been revoked.

Racial discrimination is now illegal in all public and most private venues in the United States. Few Americans now subscribe to the doctrine of separate but equal or the belief that whites are a superior race. However, many critics say that the Jim Crow policies that flourished under the protection of *Plessy v. Ferguson* remain. In *Dismantling Racism: The Continuing Challenge to White America* Joseph Barndt declares that American society is far from erasing the divisions, once legally condoned, that separate races in the United States: "Under a more sophisticated system of racism, members of the same race have no explicit restrictions on where they live, no legal limitations on their education, nor on the kind of jobs they can have. Yet, [minorities] are still undereducated, underemployed, and ghettoized."[78] These conditions, he concludes, are proof that despite the denials of many, racism still exists in this country.

The Judgment of History on *Plessy v. Ferguson*

The Supreme Court's ruling in *Plessy v. Ferguson* did not create the Jim Crow system of segregation in the South, whose effects linger to this day. Many of the customs and laws were already in place before the case began. No doubt many of the barriers to equality that were erected after the ruling would have cropped

Slums like this were common during times of segregation. Racism is now illegal, but it is still very much alive in the United States.

up without it, allowing the notion of white supremacy to hold sway over the region. But by providing legal cover for such racial discrimination, *Plessy v. Ferguson* cast the United States in the role of villain, limited citizens' options for using the legal system to secure civil rights, and made the long hard fight for equal rights more difficult.

Today, the *Plessy v. Ferguson* decision is almost universally regarded as one of the worst in the Supreme Court's history, rivaling that of the *Dred Scott* case. In fact many experts have agreed with Chief Justice Warren Burger that, "As terrible as the Dred Scott holding had been, Plessy was arguably much more condemnable inasmuch as the country had fought a civil war over the issue of slavery and had had many years to contemplate the conclusions arrived at in Dred Scott." [79]

Justice Henry Brown's majority opinion in *Plessy* has been widely criticized as weakly argued and poorly written, based on racist opinions and faulty logic. Especially harsh criticism has been reserved for Brown's statement that if the Separate Car

Law stamped blacks with a badge of inferiority it is "solely because the colored race chooses to put that construction on it." As Supreme Court biographer Timothy L. Hall notes, "For a court that had announced a generation earlier in the Dred Scott decision that blacks were so inherently inferior that they could under no circumstances qualify as U.S. citizens, this was an astounding statement." [80]

In 1995 retired Chief Justice Warren Burger spoke for many when he regarded the *Plessy* decision as a forsaking of the values upon which the United States was founded. "The lopsided decision in Plessy," said Burger, "suggests that the Court in 1896 had not learned what the Constitution really meant in terms of true human freedom." [81]

Even Brown eventually grew uncomfortable with his ruling. After his retirement from the Court, he admitted that in *Plessy v. Ferguson* and in similar cases, he and his colleagues may have sacrificed the intent of the Fourteenth Amendment to a narrow reading of the letter of the law.

Historians today, however critical of Brown's actual words, look at the decision in the context of the times. They recognize that in writing his opinion Brown was relying on racial assumptions of white superiority that were not only commonplace in the United States, but appeared to be supported by the objective scientific establishment. As one biographer says, "By voicing the racial views common to his age, [Brown] captured for one enduring historical moment the harsh glare of unfavorable attention." [82] Some historians are of the opinion that the Court had very little choice but to uphold Louisiana's law, believing that a ruling that outlawed a state's right to make distinctions between races could have led to another civil war.

Harlan's Crowning Achievement

In light of the times, and John Marshall Harlan's own background as a Southern slaveholder, this justice becomes all the more astonishing. Burger calls "the views of this one dissenter among the most eloquent utterances in the pages of public opinion." [83]

Jerrold M. Packard is of a similar opinion, writing, "Unique among prominent jurists of 1896, he understood the damage the high court's decision would do to the black man, the black man's future, and to the future of American society."[84] Demonstrating the value of impassioned eloquent dissent in a democracy, it is Harlan's view of the U.S. Constitution and not those of his seven colleagues that has come to be established as the law of the land.

Notes

Introduction: A Short but Historic Trip

1. Quoted in *Plessy v. Ferguson*, 163 U.S. 537 (1896).
2. Quoted in *Plessy v. Ferguson*, 163 U.S. 537.

Chapter 1: Freed but Equal?

3. Warren Burger, *It Is So Ordered: A Constitution Unfolds.* New York: William Morrow, 1995, p. 128.
4. Quoted in Pauline Meyer, *American Scripture.* New York: Alfred A. Knopf, 1997, p. 134.
5. C. Vann Woodward, *The Strange Career of Jim Crow.* New York: Oxford University Press, 1957, p. xiii.
6. Quoted in Langston Hughes and Milton Meltzer, *A Pictorial History of African Americans.* New York: Crown Publishers, 1970, p. 50.
7. Quoted in James W. Loewen, *Lies My Teacher Told Me.* New York: Touchstone, 1995, p. 154.
8. Quoted in Charles A. Lofgren, *The Plessy Case: A Legal-Historical Interpretation.* New York: Oxford University Press, 1987, p. 96.
9. Quoted in Lofgren, *The Plessy Case*, p. 8.
10. Quoted in Loewen, *Lies My Teacher Told Me*, p. 147.
11. Loewen, *Lies My Teacher Told Me*, p. 158.
12. Quoted in William H. Chafe et al., eds., *Remembering Jim Crow: African-Americans Tell About Life in the Segregated South.* New York: New Press, 2001, p. 44.
13. Quoted in Eric Fones, *Reconstruction: America's Unfinished Revolution, 1863–1877.* New York: Harper & Row, p. 256.
14. Quoted in Woodward, *The Strange Career of Jim Crow*, p. 21.
15. Loewen, *Lies My Teacher Told Me*, p. 157.
16. Woodward, *The Strange Career of Jim Crow*, p. 7.
17. Quoted in Hughes, *A Pictorial History of African Americans*, p. 206.

18. George Mason University—History 122, "The Civil Rights Act of 1875." www.chnm.gmu.edu.

Chapter 2: Background of the *Plessy* Case

19. Quoted in Woodward, *The Strange Career of Jim Crow*, p. xiii.
20. Quoted in Woodward, *The Strange Career of Jim Crow*, p. 70.
21. Quoted in Woodward, *The Strange Career of Jim Crow*, p. 18.
22. Quoted in Woodward, *The Strange Career of Jim Crow*, p. xvi.
23. Quoted in Chafe, *Remembering Jim Crow*, p. 72.
24. Quoted in Lofgren, *The Plessy Case*, p. 9.
25. Benjamin Arnett, "The Black Laws," *Ohio State Journal*, 1886. www.lcwebs.loc.gov.
26. Quoted in Chafe, *Remembering Jim Crow*, p. 69.
27. Quoted in Lofgren, *The Plessy Case*, p. 12.
28. Quoted in Raphael Cassimere and Caryn Ball, "From Equality to Jim Crow," Tulane University. www.tulane.edu.

Chapter 3: Louisiana's Separate Car Law Goes to Court

29. Quoted in Lofgren, *The Plessy Case*, p. 32.
30. Cassimere and Ball, "From Equality to Jim Crow."
31. Quoted in Lofgren, *The Plessy Case*, p. 180.
32. Quoted in Hughes, *A Pictorial History of African Americans*, p. 232.
33. Loewen, *Lies My Teacher Told Me*, p. 164.
34. Quoted in Terry Eastland, ed., *Great Controversies in the Supreme Court*. Grand Rapids, MI: William B. Eerdman, 1995, p. 39.
35. Quoted in Lofgren, *The Plessy Case*, p. 108.
36. George R. Stetson, *Protestant Episcopal Review*, Vassar College History Department, December 1896. www. iberie.vassar.edu.
37. Quoted in Lofgren, *The Plessy Case*, p. 157.
38. Quoted in Cassimere and Ball, "From Equality to Jim Crow."
39. Quoted in Tony Mauro, *Illustrated Decisions of the Supreme Court*. Washington, DC: CQ Press, 2000, p. 142.
40. Quoted in Leon Friedman and Fred L. Israel, *The Justices of the Supreme Court, 1789–1969: Their Lives and Major Opinions*. New Providence, NJ: R.R. Bowker, 1969, p. 29.

Chapter 4: The Supreme Court Decides

41. Quoted in Burger, *It Is So Ordered*, p. 130.
42. Legal Information Institute, "Civil Rights Act of 1870." www.law.cornell.edu.
43. *U.S. v. Cruikshank* 92 U.S. 542 (1875).
44. *U.S. v. Cruikshank* 92 U.S. 542.
45. *U.S. v. Cruikshank* 92 U.S. 542.
46. Quoted in Burger, *It Is So Ordered*, p.134.
47. *Ex Parte State of Virginia* 100 U.S. 39 (1879).
48. *Ex Parte State of Virginia* 100 U.S. 39.
49. *Strauder v. West Virginia*, 100 U.S. 303 (1879).
50. *Strauder v. West Virginia*, 100 U.S. 303.
51. Quoted in Hughes, *A Pictorial History of African Americans*, p. 268.
52. Quoted in Mauro, *Illustrated Decisions of the Supreme Court*, p. 232.
53. *Plessy v. Ferguson* 163 U.S. 537.
54. *Plessy v. Ferguson* 163 U.S. 537.
55. *Plessy v. Ferguson* 163 U.S. 537.
56. *Plessy v. Ferguson* 163 U.S. 537.
57. *Plessy v. Ferguson* 163 U.S. 537.
58. *Plessy v. Ferguson* 163 U.S. 537.
59. *Plessy v. Ferguson* 163 U.S. 537.
60. *Plessy v. Ferguson* 163 U.S. 537.
61. *Plessy v. Ferguson* 163 U.S. 537.

Chapter 5: *Plessy v. Ferguson:* Reaction and Legacy

62. *Plessy v. Ferguson* 163 U.S. 537.
63. *Plessy v. Ferguson* 163 U.S. 537.
64. *Plessy v. Ferguson* 163 U.S. 537.
65. *Plessy v. Ferguson* 163 U.S. 537.
66. *Plessy v. Ferguson* 163 U.S. 537.
67. *Plessy v. Ferguson* 163 U.S. 537.
68. *Plessy v. Ferguson* 163 U.S. 537.
69. *Plessy v. Ferguson* 163 U.S. 537.
70. Quoted in Lofgren, *The Plessy Case*, p. 19.
71. Quoted in Chafe, *Remembering Jim Crow*, p. 70.
72. Quoted in Hughes, *A Pictorial History of African Americans*, p. 268.

73. Quoted in Michael Lee Lanning, *The African-American Soldier*. Secaucus, NJ: Birch Lane, 1977, p. 211.

74. Quoted in Jon Meacham, "A Man Out of Time," *Newsweek*, December 23, 2002, p. 31.

75. Quoted in John Garrety, ed., *Quarrels That Have Shaped the Constitution*. New York: Harper & Row, 1987, p. 310.

76. Quoted in Stephen Goode, *The Controversial Court: Supreme Court Influences on American Life*. New York: Julian Messner, 1982. p. 54.

77. Quoted in Robert A. Caro, *Lyndon Johnson: Master of the Senate*. New York: Alfred A. Knopf, 2002, p. 767.

78. Joseph Barndt, *Dismantling Racism: The Continuing Challenge to White America*. Minneapolis, MN: Augsburg, 1991, p. 18.

79. Burger, *It Is So Ordered*, p. 131.

80. Timothy L. Hall, *Supreme Court Justices: A Biographical Dictionary*. New York: Facts On File, 2001, p. 209.

81. Burger, *It Is So Ordered*, p. 135.

82. Hall, *Supreme Court Justices*, p. 209.

83. Burger, *It Is So Ordered*, p. 135.

84. Jerrold M. Packard, *American Nightmare: The History of Jim Crow*. New York: St. Martin's Press, 2002, p. 77.

Timeline

1841
Massachusetts passes the first known Jim Crow law requiring separate railroad cars for blacks and whites.

1857
U.S. Supreme Court issues its ruling in the *Dred Scott* case, declaring blacks cannot be citizens.

1863
Lincoln issues Emancipation Proclamation, freeing slaves in Confederate states.

1865
States approve Thirteenth Amendment outlawing slavery.

1865–1867
Black Codes enacted by former Confederate states.

1867
Congress passes Reconstruction Act.

1868
Fourteenth Amendment protecting equal legal rights for blacks ratified.

1870
Fifteenth Amendment guaranteeing right of blacks to vote ratified.

1871
Southern states initiate the poll tax.

1875
Congress passes Civil Rights Act providing wide-ranging protection for blacks against discrimination.

1879
Last federal troops pulled out of the South, ending Reconstruction era.

1881

Tennessee becomes first state to enact discriminatory laws under the "separate but equal" wording.

1883

U.S. Supreme Court invalidates most of the Civil Rights Act of 1875.

1890

Louisiana passes Separate Car Law.

September 1, 1891

Black citizens of New Orleans organize Citizens Committee to Test the Constitutionality of the Separate Car Law.

February 24, 1892

Daniel Desdunes makes first attempt to challenge Separate Car Law.

June 7, 1892

Homer Plessy challenges the law and is arrested.

November 18, 1892

Judge John Ferguson rules against Plessy; case is appealed.

April 13, 1896

U.S. Supreme Court hears arguments in *Plessy v. Ferguson*.

May 18, 1896

Supreme Court announces its decision upholding the Louisiana law.

May 17, 1954

In *Brown v. Board of Education*, Supreme Court overturns ruling of *Plessy v. Ferguson* and bans public discrimination on the basis of race.

For Further Reading

Books

Nathan Aaseng, *You Are the Supreme Court Justice*. Minneapolis, MN: Oliver Press, 1997. Gives readers the chance to put themselves in the shoes of actual Supreme Court justices in attempting to rule on cases, including *Plessy*.

Christopher Collier, *Reconstruction and the Rise of Jim Crow, 1864–1896*. New York: Benchmark, 2000. A brief overview of the period and the relationship between Reconstruction efforts and Jim Crow law.

Charles George, *Life Under the Jim Crow Laws*. San Diego: Lucent, 2000. From The Way People Live series, this book helps readers to get a feel for how Jim Crow law affected everyday life.

Bonnie Likes, *The Dred Scott Decision*. San Diego: Lucent, 1997. A readable examination of the infamous Supreme Court decision: how it was reached, who was involved, and the far-reaching consequences.

Nick Treanor, *The Civil Rights Movement*. San Diego: Greenhaven Press, 2003. Documents more than a century of struggle for black civil rights.

Websites

African American History. (www.afroamhistory.about.com). Provides complete information and documentation of *Plessy v. Ferguson*.

Office of International Information Programs. (www.usinfo. state.gov). Includes a very detailed look at *Plessy*, with transcripts of the opinions.

Works Consulted

Books

Joseph Barndt, *Dismantling Racism: The Continuing Challenge to White America*. Minneapolis, MN: Augsburg, 1991. A controversial exposition of how the racist legacy of the United States continues to impact its citizens.

Warren Burger, *It Is So Ordered: A Constitution Unfolds*. New York: William Morrow, 1995. The chief justice appointed by Richard Nixon offers an insider's view of the Supreme Court's historic decisions.

Robert A. Caro, *Lyndon Johnson: Master of the Senate*. New York: Alfred A. Knopf, 2002. This biography of Johnson devotes a large amount of time to detailing his efforts to deal with Southern racists in Congress.

William H. Chafe et al., eds., *Remembering Jim Crow: African-Americans Tell About Life in the Segregated South*. New York: New Press, 2001. An excellent primary source for firsthand rememberances of what the Jim Crow South was like. The editors are militant civil rights advocates.

Terry Eastland, ed., *Great Controversies in the Supreme Court*. Grand Rapids, MI: William B. Eerdman, 1995. Less challenging than most books on the subject, this book includes a chapter exploring the *Plessy* case.

Eric Fones, *Reconstruction: America's Unfinished Revolution, 1863–1877*. New York: Harper & Row, 1987. The author provides an in-depth look at the Reconstruction era: what was intended and what was accomplished.

Leon Friedman and Fred L. Israel, The *Justices of the Supreme Court, 1789–1969: Their Lives and Major Opinions*. New Providence, NJ: R.R. Bowker, 1969. This book is a fine source of biographical detail on the Supreme Court justices in addition to identifying their impact and crucial decisions.

John Garrety, ed., *Quarrels That Have Shaped the Constitution*. New York: Harper & Row, 1987. Another look at selected cases with special emphasis on how they affected constitutional law.

Walter L. Fleming's *Reading the Fine Print: Grandfather Clause in Louisiana.*

Stephen Goode, *The Controversial Court: Supreme Court Influences on American Life.* New York: Julian Messner, 1982. A clear and easy way to understand the Supreme Court's rulings that have affected U.S. society.

Timothy L. Hall, *Supreme Court Justices: A Biographical Dictionary.* New York: Facts On File, 2001. An intriguing look at the lives of the justices who made such an impact on U.S. legal history.

Langston Hughes and Milton Meltzer, *A Pictorial History of African Americans.* New York: Crown Publishers, 1970. A wide-ranging view of the history of African Americans from the perspective of a famous black poet. The book includes excellent material on the Jim Crow era.

Richard Kluger, *Simple Justice: The History of Brown v. Board of Education and Black America's Struggle for Equality.* New York: Alfred A. Knopf, 1976. A very detailed and lengthy study of the famous court case that ended official sanction of the separate but equal policy.

Michael Lee Lanning, *The African-American Soldier.* Secaucus, NJ: Birch Lane, 1977. An informative history of blacks in the military in the United States and the integration of the military following World War II.

James W. Loewen, *Lies My Teacher Told Me.* New York: Touchstone, 1995. A hard-hitting, fascinating, and often disturbing account of how textbooks have tended to soften the edges of history with a particular focus on myths about the Reconstruction period.

Charles A. Lofgren, *The Plessy Case: A Legal-Historical Interpretation.* New York: Oxford University Press, 1987. The most in-depth exploration of the issues surrounding the *Plessy* case.

Tony Mauro, *Illustrated Decisions of the Supreme Court.* Washington, DC: CQ Press, 2000. This book makes good use of photographs to present some of the more controversial Supreme Court rulings, including *Plessy.*

Pauline Meyer, *American Scripture*. New York: Alfred A. Knopf, 1997. A detailed examination of the struggles and controversies involved in the writing and adopting of the Declaration of Independence.

Jerrold M. Packard, *American Nightmare: The History of Jim Crow*. New York: St. Martin's Press, 2002. A recent book exploring the impact of white supremacy in the South.

C. Vann Woodward, *The Strange Career of Jim Crow*. New York: Oxford University Press, 1957. A classic in its time, the book presents a complex view of the segregated South in the late nineteenth century.

Internet Sources

Benjamin Arnett, "The Black Laws," *Ohio State Journal*, 1886. www.lcwebs.loc.gov.

Raphael Cassimere and Caryn Ball, "From Equality to Jim Crow," Tulane University. www.tulane.edu.

George Mason University—History 122, "The Civil Rights Act of 1875." www.chnm.gmu.edu.

Legal Information Institute, "Civil Rights Act of 1870." www.law.cornell.edu.

George R. Stetson, *Protestant Episcopal Review*, Vassar College History Department, December 1896. www.iberie.vassar.edu.

Periodicals

Jon Meacham, "A Man Out of Time," *Newsweek*, December 23, 2002, p. 31.

Evan Thomas, "Race to the Exit," *Newsweek*, January 6, 2003, pp. 42–45.

Index

Picture Credits

About the Author

Nathan Aaseng, who lives in Eau Claire, Wisconsin, has written more than 160 books on a wide range of subjects. In 1999, he was recognized by the Wisconsin Library Association as a Notable Wisconsin Author.